The
Italian
Vegetable
Garden

The Complete Guide to Growing and Preparing
Traditional Italian-Style Vegetables

ROSALIND CREASY

TUTTLE Publishing

Tokyo | Rutland, Vermont | Singapore

Preface

How do I say this politely: my mother and our live-in grandmother were dreadful cooks. Especially when it came to vegetables. For one thing, most of our vegetables were frozen, or worse, canned, and they were always overcooked. Ugh, I still remember not being allowed to leave the table until I ate them. And garlic—I never tasted it until I went to college! When I questioned my English-born grandmother about garlic, she said very matter-of-factly, "We're not Italian." It was a perfect storm—we weren't Italian, my mom and grandmother didn't know how to cook, and it was Massachusetts in the 50s.

When I went off to college, I quickly learned that there was a whole world of food out there, and that I loved garlic! Of course most of it was on ubiquitous pizzas, and with pasta. That limited view changed in the early 70s when my husband and I traveled to Italy. It was clear that their cuisine was far more complex. In fact, an array of vegetables was integral to the meal, from the antipasto to the dessert; our first antipasto was cherry peppers stuffed with olives, another day it was a classic dish of "agliata," a pungent garlic sauce served on grilled vegetables, and there were the grilled radicchios and young cardoon served with bagna cauda, (a hot garlic anchovy sauce), even a dessert tart made with chard. Contrary to what I—and most Americans—believed, Italians enjoy a long and broad cuisine based on vegetables. Over the last decades, as vegetarian and vegan movements have influenced all of us to include more vegetables in our own diets, we've come to learn that the Italian diet is in fact one of the healthiest in the world.

Years ago Italian immigrants had to grow their own rich-flavored serpent garlic, "rocambole," Tuscan black kale, arugula, radicchio, and countless more vegetables because they couldn't find them in the grocery stores. In fact, they couldn't even find the seeds to grow them, so they would bring their own or have folks send them. Thankfully, times have changed, and we are in the golden age of vegetables and herbs, many of them of Italian origin. But while most markets now offer an array of Italian greens, canned San Marzano tomatoes, and the ubiquitous basil, I've yet to see many of the classics, including cardoons, purple artichokes, per-eroncini peppers, tender sprouting broccolis, rustic arugula, yellow Romano beans, Italian red garlics, much less nepetella and young dandelions. The bottom line—to really explore and enjoy authentic Italian cuisine, you need to grow many of these vegetables yourself.

The great news is that over the last few decades dozens of dedicated seeds people, frustrated with the mainline vegetable seed companies and their meager Italian offerings, have started seed companies that specialize in Italian vegetables and herbs. Further, the now-popular heirloom movement has opened up vast seed libraries and seed swaps of classic Italian specialties. Never before have we had this much opportunity to explore one of the world's greatest cuisines! With this book in hand you too can glory in a spring patch of wild Italian greens and show off a bountiful patio container of slim tender Italian eggplants and nepitella for a classic grilled eggplant and nepitella butter. And of course your trellis of San Marzano tomatoes will produce enough for many a killer pasta sauce.

Bon Appetito!

Rosalind Greasy

author Rosalind Creasy

Contents

The Italian Garden

My taxi driver in Rome was sure it was a mistake and sent me back into the hotel to have someone translate the note I had handed him. It was six o'clock in the morning, and my note said, in Italian, "Please take me to the Rome produce market." Once there, I understood immediately why the driver thought I had made a mistake. The place was alive with people, occasional verbal abuse was being exchanged, purveyors pushed dollies and jockeyed for position, and utter chaos reigned. I was a little on edge, but after one glimpse at the stacks of spectacular and unfamiliar vegetables everywhere in sight, I relaxed. I had dedicated more than ten years to edible plants, and it was exciting to see some I didn't know. And now I'd find out why vegetables and fruits I'd been eating in restaurants throughout Italy had been so outstanding.

RIGHT: Baby artichokes, romanesco type broccolis, and ruby heads of radicchios (right) are domesticated versions of plants that have been used in Italy since ancient times. Another such plant, the Judas tree or European red bud (*Cercis siliquastrum*), shown here, blooms in spring, and the magenta blossoms are enjoyed raw in Italy in salads or pickled in vinegar.

I was intimidated at first by all the shouting, but within minutes the passion both vendors and buyers showed for the produce put me at ease. Besides, how can a food lover be cool in front of a waist-high pile of purple artichokes? The men beamed at my continued delight as I wandered through the stalls and exclaimed over sculptured chartreuse broccoli, purple cauliflower, and stalks of miniature fava bean plants covered with pink flowers. "Do you eat the leaves and the flowers?" I tried to

ask, eliciting shrugs and loud laughter. I wondered about the contorted stems of what looked like celery (the chicory 'Catalogna Puntarella,' I found out later) and marveled over bright magenta spheres. "Radicchio!" the vendor cried. We all exchanged fabulous gestures as I tried to put English words to vegetables and varieties I'd never seen before.

Prior to my first trip to Italy almost thirty-five years ago, Italian vegetables had meant mostly zucchini and tomatoes to me. The herbs were garlic and basil, and Italian cuisine was primarily pizza and spaghetti. Now I know that while these items are Italian, they make up only a small part of the cuisine—mostly from southern Italy. I learned about marinated vegetables—bright red peppers and sweet onions with fennel, all bathed in olive oil and herbs. I came to love deep-fried cardoon (a close relative of the artichoke) and to savor slices of sweet cantaloupe wrapped with prosciutto, as well as *bagna cauda*, a vast range of raw vegetables dipped in cream and olive oil flavored with anchovies and garlic. I consumed loads of pesto and memorable salads made with endive, tangy arugula, and radicchio. And the pasta! I sampled sauces far more imaginative than our nearly mandatory tomato sauce. In Italy pasta is made in a wide variety of shapes and might be served with a cream sauce and crowned with fresh baby peas or string beans. What revelations! What bliss!

I returned from Italy filled with enthusiasm and, already missing the food, determined to track down the vegetables and herbs I had seen and to learn how to cook them. I visited Italian markets, perused specialty seed catalogs, and interviewed Italian gardeners. The latter two sources yielded the most information. A love of gardening is part of the Italian heritage, which, together with frustration at the limited selection and quality of supermarket vegetables, had inspired many of the Italian Americans I met to plant extensive gardens filled with unusual vegetables. Many of the owners of the specialty seed companies similarly started their businesses out of a frustration with the limited availability of varieties of European seeds in the United States. They had discovered the Italian vegetables and were as excited about them as I was.

No wonder Americans, using supermarket produce that often tastes like the cardboard it's packaged in, simply can't duplicate the "taste of Italy." Americans might have recently discovered balsamic vinegar and fresh mozzarella, and some American gourmets are spending eight dollars a pound on radicchio, but many Italian specialties

such as cardoon, the spicy rustic arugula, leaf chicories, broccoli raab, purple artichokes that can be eaten raw, the melting yellow romano beans, and the mellow mint nepitella are still not available. It looks as though anyone who wants to experience the rich spectrum of tastes of true Italian cooking is still going to have to plant a garden!

OPPOSITE: Like in much of Europe, small farmers' markets are very popular in Italy. The number and quality of similar markets in the United States is growing quickly, and they are great places for gardeners to learn more about vegetable varieties that grow well in their climates.
BELOW: A woman strings cherry tomatoes in preparation for drying. Drying is the most common use for cherry tomatoes in Italy, and it is most associated with the hot, arid, areas in the south.

How to Grow an Italian Garden

The majority of vegetables and herbs planted in an Italian vegetable garden, and the methods for growing them, are very similar to the crops and methods used in most gardens. In Italy small plots of ground are cultivated near the home, and individual vegetables are most often grown in rows. Many of the vegetables are comfortably familiar to us, namely, tomatoes, beans, zucchini, cucumbers, eggplant, broccoli, lettuce, and peppers. In fact, sometimes they grow the identical variety.

But as a rule, Italians grow slightly different varieties of our favorite vegetables. The Italian tomato varieties are most often paste types, the sweet peppers are frequently long and thin rather than short and blocky, the green beans are often flat romano types or curved anellinos, and the eggplants are generally smaller and either elongated or round. In addition, in Italy gardeners grow a number of vegetables and herbs that are less common here: including Tuscan black kale (lacinato); many kinds of cutting and heading chicories; borlotto-type, pink-striped shelling beans; large flat and purple artichokes; 'Tromboncino,' elongated squashes; sweet fennel; all sorts of greens; and many varieties of large- and small-leafed basils. (And while not easily grown, another Italian favorite, capers, can be grown here in mild climates.)

This harvest includes Italian parsley; basil; paste and the fluted, flat 'Costoluto Genovese' tomatoes; 'Milano' zucchini; 'Violetta Lunga' eggplant; and 'Rossa di Milano' and 'Giallo di Milano' onions.

In addition, Italians harvest many plants from the wild and grow some of them in their gardens. Italian gardeners grow and harvest "baby greens" and garden blanch (deprive the plants of light to make them more tender and less bitter) many of the chicories, endive, and cardoon.

To enjoy many of the Italian specialties in your own garden, you must order both the Italian varieties of common vegetables and the more unusual vegetables and herbs from specialty seed companies. See Resources (page 109) for the names and urls of seed companies and nurseries.

Because Italy is on the Mediterranean, its climate is characterized by long, hot summers with very little rain, fairly mild winters, and a long spring and fall. The long growing season allows the Italian gardener to plant slow-maturing plants, such as some of the radicchios, many garlic varieties, and some varieties of sweet peppers; to plant vegetables that grow best in a long, cool spring, such as fava beans and cardoon; to enjoy the tender perennial artichoke; and to sun-dry tomatoes with ease. In the United States a similar climate is found in parts of California, Texas, Arizona, and New Mexico. American gardeners in other states who want to grow these plants sometimes must make cultural compromises. Gardeners in the humid South need to plant especially disease-resistant varieties and will have the most success if they provide afternoon shade for species that suffer in the heat. Gardeners

LEFT: One of my early specialty gardens included many vegetables and herbs enjoyed in Italy. The beds were filled with tall, purple sprouting broccolis, beets, chard, arugula, chicories, and lettuces as well as rosemary, oregano, fennel, thyme, and parsley.

RIGHT: Nothing is healthier or more flavorful than vegetables, harvested at their peak, that have gone fresh from the garden to the kitchen and table.

BELOW RIGHT: A selection of fresh vegetables featuring varieties of onions, peppers, and the tomatoes for which Italy is famous.

at high altitudes and in cool northern areas will do beautifully with some of the spring and fall vegetables but need to provide extra heat for tomatoes, peppers, melons, and eggplant. Here black plastic mulches, windbreaks, south-facing masonry walls, and floating row covers help raise the ambient temperature by 5°–10°F/-15° to -12.2°C.

I find that to fully appreciate any garden or cooking situation enough to write about it, I need to grow and cook with most of the featured plants. To this end, I have enthusiastically grown and cooked with hundreds of Italian vegetables and herbs and visited many sumptuous gardens. I offer you my own experiences with these wonderful varieties in the pages that follow.

Picking & Growing Wild Greens

It is difficult to delve into Italian cooking without coming across references to foraging and serving wild greens and herbs. Generations of Italians have stayed close to the land, often under very lean conditions. For their survival, and because many outlying towns remained isolated, rural Italians continued to harvest from the wild after much of Europe had ceased doing so. For many years this practice had little status, and the plants gathered, like borage and mustard, were considered peasant food. Nowadays upscale restaurants serve many of these "wild" greens, and it's not unusual to find market stalls in Italy offering them too. Some of the greens are still gathered from the wild, but more often they are grown in market gardens. Italian cookbooks also call for wild greens these days, and proponents all over the world see consuming these nutrition-packed greens—whether grown domestically or in the wild—as a part of a healthy lifestyle. Even though some of these greens are not widely available outside of Italy, as a gardener you are in the fortunate position of being able to grow most of them yourself. Further, gardeners are better able to gather plants from the wild because they have the skills to recognize different species more readily than does a nongardener.

A home garden in Italy backs up to the Alps. In this cooler climate, summer gardens include broccoli, lettuces, leeks, onions, cabbages, and fava beans.

"Wild greens" (**CLOCKWISE FROM TOP LEFT**) are borage, violets, sorrel, nepitella, purslane, nasturtiums, corn salad (mâche), and wild lettuce; rows of young nasturtiums and chicories (**OPPOSITE BOTTOM**) are ready for harvest as "wild greens."

These plants may be uncommon in markets, but it's not because they are hard to grow. After all, they grow untended in many parts of the world. In fact, give some of them a chance and they can become thugs and crowd out their weaker domestic cousins. As a gardener, you probably already know a few "up close and personal," namely, dandelions and purslane (one of the pigweeds).

Over the years there have been dozens of plants associated with wild harvesting, some used as pot-herbs or vegetables, others used raw in salads. In Italian these plants are referred to as *erbe selvatiche.* The more familiar ones include arugula (*Eruca vesicaria, Diplotaxis tenuifolia*); borage (*Borago officinalis);* burnet (*Sanguisorba minor);* the many chicories (*Cichorium* sp.); the cresses (*Barbarea verna, Nasturtium officinalis*); dandelion (T*araxacum officinale*); fennel (*Foeniculum vulgare*); corn salad, also called mâche and lamb's lettuce (*Valerianella locusta*); hops (*Humulus lupulus*); mustard (*Brassica nigra*); nasturtiums (*Tropaeolum majus*); purslane (*Portulaca oleracea* var. *sativa*); salsify (*Tragopogon porrifolius*); sorrel (*Rumex acetosa*);

and violets (*Viola odorata*). The more esoteric ones include chickweed (*Stellaria media*); Good-King-Henry (*Chenopodium bonus-henricus*); nepitella, also called calamint (*Calamintha nepeta*); minutina, also called *erba stella* and buck's horn plantain (*Plantago coronopus*); shepherd's purse (*Capsella bursa-pastoris*); silene (*Silene vulgaris*); mallow (*Malva* sp.); alexanders or black lovage (*Smyrnium olusatrum*); rampion (*Campanula rapun-culus);* samphire (*Crithmum maritimum*); and nettles (*urtica dioica*), which must be cooked so the multitudinous prickly hairs on the leaves are softened.

Historically, these wild greens were a welcome sight in the spring after a long winter of meals that were devoid of fresh edible leaves. The greens were consumed as a "tonic" to cleanse the system but were also enjoyed as a treat to the palate and for the senses after a gray winter. In fact, Italians who move to the city or away from Italy speak fondly of them. Italian chef Celestino Drago, who operates three restaurants and a bakery in Los Angeles, would make an annual pilgrimage to his home in Sicily. If he and his brothers couldn't make the trip in early spring, their mom would make sure they could still enjoy the taste of the first flush of young wild greens, which she would lovingly cook or steam, drain and freeze until her sons could come home to her table. In the spring, when the California hills are covered with wild mustard, Drago would gather this potherb and continue the culinary tradition by preparing it for his family in several ways: as a simple vegetable, sautéed with garlic and olive oil; combined with a tomato sauce and spooned over pasta; or in risotto.

Seeds for many of the species mentioned above are available from specialty nurseries, but seeds for those plants known only as garden weeds (like shepherd's purse and chickweed) may take a little more effort.

So let's start with the easiest way to obtain these greens—seeing which ones are already growing wild in the fields and woods or growing as weeds in your garden. Obviously, these plants need to be identified properly. Use a field guide, such as the *Peterson Field Guide to Edible Wild Plants*; better yet, go out in the wild with someone who knows the plants (just as with mushrooms, a number of wild plants are poisonous). Keep in mind that common names are different all over the world, so use only the Latin names. Personally, I find Roger Phillips's *Wild Food* a great help in identifying plants; it has many photos. Another helpful resource is the venerable *Complete Book of Fruits and Vegetables*, by a number of Italian botanists.

If you are gathering your greens from the wild, make sure they're not growing by a heavily traveled road (to prevent lead contamination) and avoid rights-of-way that may have been sprayed with herbicides. The best time to forage is in the spring because all these greens need to be harvested when they are young or, if they are perennial plants, when they are producing new shoots and leaves. Very young plants or shoots are tender enough to be used raw in salads, but completely mature leaves are tough and bitter or acrid. Between the newest young shoots and the tough mature leaves is an in-between stage when the leaves are great cooked and used in soups or sauces;

as fillings for a frittata, calzone, or torta; and as a topping on pizzas. They can also be blanched and made into nests that can be filled with cheese or eggs.

Growing a Misticanza Garden

The most common way to enjoy wild greens is in a *misticanza*, the Italian term for a combination of a variety of young, tender, and sweet leaves. Its French counterpart is called *mesclun*. However, in today's restaurant vernacular, either mixture may in fact be just a mixed green salad containing many different lettuces and edible flowers—a far cry from freshly harvested young leaves in a combination of tastes and textures. According to Anna Del Conte in *Gastronomy of Italy*, "Roman gastronomes think a classic *misticanza* should include 21 different types of wild greens. . . . These include: arugula, sorrel, mint, radichella—a kind of dandelion—lamb's lettuce, purslane, and other local edible weeds." Some of us think that's a bit extreme and settle for half a dozen or so.

The techniques for growing both an Italian *misticanza* and a French *mesclun* are identical. As few of us have all sorts of wild greens growing near our home, fortunately, there are prepackaged combinations of seeds for a traditional Italian *misticanza* available from specialty seed companies. For instance, Johnny's Selected Seeds (www.johnny seeds.com) offers quite a selection of chicories and lettuces. Or you can mix your own combination

of plants in which different tastes—for example, spicy, nutty, sweet, mild, and bitter—or different textures play off one another. As a note: Most of the seeds for the greens available from specialty growers are semi-domesticated; therefore, the plants will be more tender and succulent compared with foraged plants such as wild dandelion or chicory.

Growing a *misticanza* garden is easy and quick and is a rewarding way to start growing your own salad greens. Unlike large lettuces grown in rows in a traditional vegetable garden, you sow *misticanza* greens in a small patch and harvest them when the plants are very young (or if they are perennials, using only the newest shoots and leaves). One thing to keep in mind when choosing plants for your *misticanza* plot is to plant

perennials in a separate location, for they will quickly outgrow the baby greens bed. Harvest your greens by plucking their young leaves as they are produced. An easy mix of plants for *misticanza* that is easy to start and maintain with the "cut-and-come-again" method of harvesting would consist of several baby lettuces of your choice, such as looseleaf 'Lollo Rossa' and the tender, small-leafed 'Biondo Liscio,' minutina; and two of the cutting chicories, 'Ceriolo' and 'Catalogna Frastagliata.' Another tasty blend is cress, arugula, the Catalonian cutting chicories 'Dentarella' and 'Spadona,' and several sweet baby lettuces such as baby romaine and salad bowl.

A *misticanza* bed can be grown in the spring or early fall. Choose a well-drained site that receives at least six hours of midday sun. Mark out an area

Gudi Riter steps away from her recipe testing to plant a small bed of baby salad greens, often called misticanza or mesclun, in my front garden. First (**ABOVE LEFT**) the soil is prepared by applying four inches of compost, and a few cups of blood and bone meal, and working them into the soil with a spading

fork. Once the soil is light and fluffy and the nutrients are incorporated, the seeds from a prepackaged mesclun mix are sprinkled lightly over the soil so that the seeds average ½ inch apart. A half inch or so of light soil or compost is then sprinkled over the bed (**ABOVE RIGHT**) and the seeds

about 10 feet by 4 feet (3 m by 1.2 m)—a generous space for a small family. Dig the area well and cover the bed with compost and manure to a depth of 3–4 inches (8–10 cm). Sprinkle the bed with a pound (454 g) or so of blood meal or hoof and horn meal and work all the amendments into the soil. Rake the bed smooth to remove clods and rocks, and you are ready to plant.

Mix the seeds in a small bowl if you are making your own *misticanza* mix. Sprinkle the seeds over the bed as you would grass seeds—try to space them about ½ inch (13 mm) apart. Sprinkle fluffy soil or compost over the bed, pat it down, and water the bed in well, being careful not to wash away the seeds. If you have problems with birds or there are many cats in the neighborhood, cover the bed with a floating row cover or bird netting.

Anchor stakes in the corners of the beds and tie the netting to them so it is a few inches off the ground. Secure the sides of the row cover or netting with scrap lumber or bricks.

Keep the soil moist until seedlings emerge in seven to ten days. Pull any weeds, but no thinning is necessary. Keep the bed fairly moist, and, depending on the weather, you will have harvestable *misticanza* greens in six to eight weeks. Either pick individual leaves by hand or take kitchen shears and cut across the bed about an inch (2.5 cm) above the crowns of the plants. Cut only the amount you want at each harvest. If the weather is favorable, in the 40°–70°F/4.4°–21.1°C range, and you keep the bed moist and apply a little fish emulsion fertilizer, the greens will regrow and you can harvest *misticanza* again in a few weeks.

and the compost are patted down to assure that the seeds are in contact with the soil. A label that includes the name of the seed mix and the date is pushed into the soil (**ABOVE LEFT**). The seeds are than gently watered in with a watering can until the soil is thoroughly moist. A piece of floating row cover (**ABOVE RIGHT**) is then applied to prevent critters from destroying the bed. To make sure the row cover won't blow away, and critters can't get in under it, the row cover is secured tightly by putting bricks or such at the corners, and along the edges if bird problems are severe.

Garden Blanching Vegetables

Another aspect of Italian gardening that deserves special attention is garden blanching vegetables, sometimes referred to as "forcing."

Garden blanching vegetables (as opposed to kitchen blanching vegetables in a pot of boiling water) is a technique whereby light is excluded from all or part of the growing vegetable to mitigate its strong taste. Vegetables that have been blanched are lighter in color and in most cases more tender than nonblanched ones. Vegetables most commonly blanched are asparagus, cardoon, cauliflower, celery, dandelions, some lettuces, and the chicories, including Belgian endive (Witloof chicory), radicchio, escarole, and curly endive (frisée).

We can trace the concept of blanching back several centuries to the time when vegetables were more closely related to their primitive ancestors—which meant they were often tough, stringy, and bitter. Blanching made them both less strong tasting and more tender. Nowadays, most modern varieties are more refined and seldom need blanching, and because forced vegetables are less nutritious and take more hand labor, they are generally less favored. So why blanch vegetables? Basically, because some vegetables have yet to be completely civilized. Cardoon, some radicchios, escarole, dandelions, and some heirloom varieties of celery and cauliflower are all preferable blanched, and Belgian endive can be eaten no other way. And sometimes gardener-cooks blanch vegetables simply to alter the taste for a treat. Thus, for elegant salads, one might blanch endive to make its curly leaves light green and sweet in the center, or dandelion leaves to make them creamy colored, tender, and less bitter.

The blanching process consists of blocking light from the part of the vegetable you plan to eat, be it leaf, stem, or shoot. The blockage keeps chlorophyll from forming, and the vegetable part will therefore be white, very pale, or, in the case of red vegetables, pink. In most cases blanched vegetables are more tender than nonblanched ones.

A few general principles cover most blanching techniques. First, you must be careful to prevent the vegetable from rotting, since the process can create fungus problems. Select only unbruised, healthy plants and make sure not to keep the plants too moist. Such vegetables as cardoon and celery need air circulation around the stalks. Make sure you blanch only a few plants at a time and stagger your harvest because most vegetables are fragile and keep poorly once they have been blanched. Thus, you would not blanch your whole crop of cardoon, escarole, or endive at one time. After you harvest your blanched vegetables, keep them in a dark place, or they will turn green again and lose the very properties you worked to achieve.

Let's go through the blanching process in detail first with a vegetable that *must* be blanched to be edible—Belgian endive.

In the fall cut off the tops of the plants to within an inch (2.5 cm) of the crown and dig up the roots. Once the plants are out of the ground, cut back the roots to 8–10 inches (20–25 cm). Bury the roots in a bucket in about a foot (0.3 m) of damp sand, packing them fairly close together. Store the roots in a dark cellar where it stays between 40° and 50°F/4.4° and 10°C. Check occasionally to make sure the sand stays moist; water sparingly when it gets dry. Within a month or so the crowns will start to resprout and produce "chicons" (the forced shoots), which you harvest when they get to be 4 or 5 inches (10 or 13 cm) tall. (The newest varieties maintain a tight head without being held in place by sand. Old varieties must have 4 or 5 inches (10 or 13 cm) of damp sand packed around the new shoots to hold them in a tight chicon.) The plants usually resprout at least once, and sometimes you can harvest them a third or fourth time. Some of the "forcing" radicchios can be blanched in the same way. In mild-winter areas both types of chicories can be blanched in the garden. Start the plants in midsummer, cut them back to the crown in early fall, build a temporary wooden box around the bed, and blanch them by covering the garden bed with 6–8 inches (15–20 cm) of sand.

To blanch celery (**TOP**), the stems are kept from sunlight for a few weeks. Here traditional terra cotta forms are used, but a wrapping of black plastic would also work. Cardoons are blanched in a similar manner. Curly endive (**ABOVE RIGHT**) can be blanched by being held in a tight head with a rubber band or string. This method also works for escarole, dandelions, and cauliflower. Heading chicories (**RIGHT**) grow in loose heads when young. Once mature, some of the older varieties must be cut back at the crown. They will soon start to resprout (**BELOW**) and form a tight head.

The preferred way to blanch cardoon stalks is to wrap the stalks with burlap or straw, surround the bundles with black plastic, and then tie them with string.

To blanch cauliflower, after the curds start to show through the leaves, gather the leaves and tie them up with soft string or plastic strips to cover the emerging head. Other vegetables can be blanched in a somewhat similar way. Blanch dandelions by loosely tying up the leaves and covering the plant with a flowerpot for a week or so, or cover the bed with 4 or 5 inches (10 or 13 cm) of sand. The flowerpot process also works well with some of the leaf chicories and is occasionally used for romaine lettuce.

Serve these blanched vegetables with ceremony and give them special treatment. Most are quite mild and are best featured with light sauces and, because they are so tender, short cooking times.

Interview:

The Sebastiani Vegetable Garden

Vicki Sebastiani is a former co-owner of Viansa Winery in the Sonoma Valley of California. Vicki has been a vegetable gardener since the age of four. I visited Vicki a number of years ago to see her garden, renowned for its beauty and bounty. When I spoke with her, Vicki's garden contained a hundred varieties of vegetables and herbs (most of them Italian), including red and yellow varieties of Italian tomatoes, white eggplant, Italian yellow and light green zucchini, giant cauliflower, variegated and red chicories, and her favorite, yellow romano beans.

Vicki's vegetable garden was a special place. It was designed with long stone planter boxes arranged in a somewhat informal oval-shaped area. The garden had benches and wrought-iron archways planted with scarlet runner beans and was bordered by a low stone wall and rose garden on one side and an inlaid stone patio and a small pond on the other. The vegetable garden was the focal point of the area, and visitors enjoyed wandering through the garden as well as viewing it from the patio tables when dining. Vicki said that most people had never seen many of the vegetables she grew.

To plant her Italian vegetable garden, said Vicki, "In late winter I send away to specialty seed companies for authentic varieties of Italian vegetable seeds. I order my American varieties from both large, well-known seed companies and small com-

Vicki Sebastiani's garden in the Sonoma Valley of California. It's mid-summer, and the tomatoes and beans are in full production and the cutting chicories and chard are filling in ready for the fall harvest.

ABOVE: The garden is located off the patio. The raised stone planters and archway make it an elegant setting for entertaining. The beds contain the last of the spring peas, leeks, onions, and many varieties of eggplants. Scarlet runner beans grow over the archway.
RIGHT: Vicki harvests cardoon, a close relative of the artichoke. Instead of eating the flower buds of this dramatic plant, the succulent stems are enjoyed.

panies that carry heirloom and hard-to-find varieties, and I glean the Italian varieties from some of the large American companies, plus poring over some of the specialty seed company catalogs. I purchased a few of the Italian varieties when I was in Italy and ordered others from an Italian seed company, Fratelli Ingegnoli."

To get a jump on the season, Vicki would start her tomatoes, peppers, eggplant, squash, basil, chicories, and cardoon in flats early in the spring so that she could transplant them into the garden after all chance of frost has passed. As the soil started to warm up in spring, she would plant the seeds of some of the early vegetables, such as lettuce, beets, carrots, fava beans, endive, arugula, and fennel. In early summer she'd start the leaf chicories for fall harvest, and a little later the broccolis for the next spring harvest.

The plants in Vicki's garden reflected a rich heritage of vegetables that are at the heart of Italian cuisine. To give you an idea of this vast range of vegetables, as well as the huge selection of Italian

varieties unfamiliar to Americans, these are some of her favorites: romanesco broccoli, both the bronze and the chartreuse types; a purple spouting broccoli; 'Pepperoncini' peppers for pickling; 'Roma' and 'San Marzano' tomatoes for sauce; white and green varieties of pattypan squash; black salsify; the peppery arugula; many chicories, including 'Palla Rossa,' 'Castelfranco,' 'Treviso,' and a Catalonian type; three varieties of Italian chard; white and purple eggplant; Italian parsley; yellow and green romano beans; and a type of large vining zucchini that produces long, meaty fruits with almost no seeds.

For many years Vicki used her garden vegetables for everyday eating, as well as for the many visitors at the winery. The vegetables would become part of an antipasto or minestrone or, in many cases, are simply steamed or boiled lightly and served with olive oil and Parmesan cheese. As Vicki said,"When you start with superior vegetables picked at the peak of perfection, they're very special in themselves."

Italian Garden Encyclopedia

Famous as Italian cuisine is for its meats and cheeses, it is based first and foremost on its fresh vegetables and fruits, offering tasty options for vegetarian and vegan meals and providing the lion's share of nutrients and flavor to dishes containing meat. Listed below are some of the most popular Italian vegetables, along with recommended varieties. I give both the Italian and Latin names in case you want to select seeds from an Italian catalog. Fratelli Ingegnoli of Milan (www.ingegnoli.it) has an extensive catalog written in English as well as Italian. Pagano is a wholesale source of Italian seeds distributed by Lake Valley Seed (www.lakevalleyseed.com) in Italian markets throughout the country. I have included a few varieties of vegetables and herbs available only from Ingegnoli and Pagano; the vast majority, however, are available from the American seed companies listed in Resources (page 109). There is much overlap between the gardens and cooking of Italy and France. I have not covered in this book some of the vegetables that are enjoyed in Italy, since they are covered in great detail in my book *The Edible French Garden*, including mâche, asparagus, melons, sorrel, leeks, and carrots.

Italian cuisine is unadorned. Food is prepared with a minimum of sauces, soufflés and other multi-layered techniques. Its strengths lie in using the very best ingredients, especially fresh, succulent vegetables picked in their prime, presented in a simple manner. A layout (**LEFT**) of just-harvested zucchinis, complete with their still-open blossoms; ripe tomatoes; fresh 'Piccolo Verde Fino' basil; eggplants; and baby leeks could be the spectacular foundation of just such an Italian meal.

ARTICHOKES, GLOBE
(carciofi) Cynara scolymus

Probably no vegetable is more typically Italian than the artichoke. There are dozens of varieties, and Italians cook these thistle buds in endless ways—far beyond serving them whole and dipping them in butter. Gardeners lucky enough to have many plants can let a few buds develop into massive blue-purple thistles that are extremely showy.

HOW TO GROW: Six plants should be ample for the average family. These large 4-foot-tall (1.2 m) dramatic plants prefer cool, moist summers and mild winters but grow in summer heat if the soil is kept continually moist. Below 28°F/-2.2°C they need winter protection, for example, an overturned basket filled with leaves or straw and placed above the roots. In coldest-winter areas artichokes are usually not successful unless the roots are brought inside during the winter and kept moist

Purple and green artichokes

and cool. In hot, early summers the artichoke buds open too soon and are tough. Artichokes prefer full sun in cool-summer areas and partial shade in hot-summer climates.

Start plants when they are bare root when possible. Plants are sold in some nurseries when they are dormant, with their roots wrapped in plastic. They are sold in nurseries in mild-winter areas of the West and in mail-order catalogs in the spring. Artichokes can be started by seeds. Sow them indoors eight weeks before your last spring frost date, about ¼ inch (6 mm) deep and ¼ inch (6 mm) apart. The soil temperature should be between 70° and 80°F/21.1° and 26.7°C Transplant seedlings to 4-inch (10 cm) pots. Grow at cooler temperatures (60°–70°F/15.5°–21.1°C during the day, 50°–60°F/10°–15.5°C at night). Transplant them to the garden when they're six to eight weeks old. (They need at least 250 hours of temperatures under 50°F/10°C to induce budding.) Protect them from frost.

Artichokes require rich, constantly moist but well-drained soil with plenty of organic matter. They respond well to deep mulches, compost, and manure. Extra nitrogen should be added halfway through the growing season and after the harvest. The plants need to be dug up and thinned every three or four years.

Aphids, earwigs, and snails are sometimes a problem. In commercial artichoke-growing areas the plume moth is a problem treated with *Bacillus thuringiensis* (Bt) applied to the center of the plants when they're moist.

To harvest artichokes, cut off the young buds about 4–6 inches (10–15 cm) below the bud (the tops of the stems are edible if peeled) before they start to open. The younger the bud, the more tender it is and the more of it is edible. The small lateral buds are also edible and if harvested while young have no choke. An unseasonable frost can brown the outer leaves of artichokes but improves the flavor.

VARIETIES
Many regions of Italy seem to have their own varieties, but few are available to outsiders. The three

described below are the only ones readily available in America.

Green Globe: most common variety grown in the United States, large conical shape, hardy throughout most of the coastal West, most available variety sold as bare root plants

Imperial Star: 90–100 days from transplants, thornless, sweet flavor, meaty hearts and almost chokeless, easiest to grow from seed and harvest the first season

Violetto: produces purple medium-size artichokes, cooking more than two minutes turns them green

Artichokes

HOW TO PREPARE: Artichokes are rich and sweet flavored, with a meaty texture, and the flavors stimulate salivation. Elsewhere, the bud is usually served whole, but in Italy young buds are often cut into pieces or pureed.

Most mature and commercial artichokes must have the choke (fuzzy, inedible center) removed. Homegrown ones, however, similar to those available in Italy, can be harvested while still young and be eaten without removing the choke.

To prepare an artichoke, cut the top inch or so off to remove any thorns and the inedible top part of the "leaves." You can leave 4–6 inches (10–15 cm) of the stem and peel it to remove the tough outer skin. Then with your fingers peel back the outside layer of leaves to where they break readily, revealing yellowish flesh at the base. Open the artichoke; if there is a fuzzy choke at the bottom, scrape it out with a sharp spoon. Immediately rub all cut edges with lemon juice (or soak them in acidulated water until you are ready to serve or cook the artichoke).

Whole artichokes can be stuffed and baked, steamed, or boiled in water with the juice of two lemons. In Rome they are sometimes braised in olive oil, garlic, and mint and served upside down with 4–6 inches (10–15 cm) of stem sticking up in the air. In all cases artichokes are cooked until a knife inserted into the bottom of the choke comes out clean. They can be presented whole, and can be accompanied with plain or flavored olive oil for dipping. To eat a whole artichoke, pull off the outside leaves and use your teeth to scrape out the flesh. Cut the remaining heart, or bottom, into bite-size pieces and relish it.

In Italy artichokes are also incorporated into many cooked dishes. Very young and tender buds are lightly trimmed and used whole or cut up. If the bud is more mature, the outside leaves and tough outer material is removed, the meaty center is quartered, and the choke is removed. Cut-up pieces are then cooked with other vegetables such as asparagus, fava beans, or peas and served as a side dish (as they do in Sicily) or combined with tomatoes and served over pasta (as is popular in many parts of southern Italy). Morsels of artichokes are added to pizza; combined with marjoram, parsley, and garlic in frittatas; incorporated into risotto and pasta sauces; and included in a creamy tart of puff pastry (as they serve it in Genoa); or pureed and made into a spread for bread or folded into soufflés. When fried whole, artichokes can be flattened out to look like a star and then fried again, as is done in the Jewish Quarter of Rome.

Young, tender artichokes are a treat when eaten raw. Pieces are dipped in olive oil as part of an antipasto; in *pinzimonio*, raw artichokes are sliced paper thin and served in olive oil, salt, and pepper.

ARUGULA
(rucola) Eruca vesicaria

RUSTIC ARUGULA
(rucola selvatica, wild arugula)
E. selvatica
(Diplotaxis tenuifolia)

Arugula leaves are lobed, pungent, and nutty and taste a bit like horseradish. The most common arugula is the domesticated milder one; however, there is another, usually called rustic arugula, that is perennial and has a more intense flavor.

HOW TO GROW: The standard arugula is grown in cool weather in early spring and again in the fall. The plants are short-lived; they get quite spicy and will go to seed in hot weather. Rustic arugula is a tender perennial, that, if started in spring and kept cut back, grows throughout the summer and fall and even winters over in mild-winter areas. Common arugula is planted in the fall for a winter harvest in these same mild climates. For both types, broadcast seeds over rich soil in a sunny area of the garden and lightly cover them with soil, or plant them in flats for transplanting into the garden. In cold climates, in the fall, plant common arugula in a cold frame or green house for winter salads. For succulent growth keep arugula well watered and fertilize lightly. Both arugulas have few pest and disease problems. Harvest individual leaves or cut back the plant and leave a few inches of growth for a cut-and-come-again crop. Common arugula comes back more quickly than the rustic one. Arugula flowers attract beneficial insects, so I keep them blooming for much of the spring. If allowed to go to seed, both arugulas reseed readily in your garden and behave as "wild greens."

VARIETIES
Arugula: 40 days, lobed green leaves, plants grow to 1 foot (0.3 m) tall, white flowers
Wild Rustic Arugula (Italian wild arugula, Sylvetta): 55 days, finely cut leaves, plants grow to 8 inches (20 cm), yellow flowers

HOW TO PREPARE: When only 2 or 3 inches (5 or 8 cm) tall, and still very mild, arugula leaves can be used in fairly large amounts to add a peppery and nutty flavor to a mixed green salad, *misticanza*, or a bread salad. Combine them with other assertive greens, especially the fall and winter ones, like chicories and mustards, and complement them with strong cheeses, capers, prosciutto, anchovies, olives, and fruit. Sprinkle young leaves of arugula over a plate of carpaccio or sliced tomatoes and serve with paper-thin fennel drizzled with olive oil, or put them in a sandwich instead of lettuce. Boiled potatoes dressed with olive oil and garlic and sprinkled with arugula and other herbs make a wonderful dish.

Arugula

Parboiled arugula can be sautéed with anchovies, garlic, and olive oil or combined with cooked white beans and served over pasta. Arugula leaves can be added to pizzas, frittatas, and soups. When the leaves become more pungent, use arugula sparingly as an herb in a mixed salad, sauce, or dressing. Long after the leaves have become too strong to use, the flowers are great in salads or as a garnish.

Sweet basil

BASIL
(basilico) Ocimum basilicum

Basil is an annual herb that glories in hot weather and withers after a light frost.

HOW TO GROW: Plant basil in a sunny site in fertile, well-drained soil with a high amount of organic matter. Start basil seeds inside a month before your weather warms up in spring or use transplants from the nursery. Keep the plants fairly moist during the growing season. If your soil is not very fertile, feed every six weeks. Harvest the leaves by hand or with scissors. Keep the flower heads continually cut back, or the plant will go to seed and give you few leaves.

VARIETIES
Fine Green (Piccolo Verde Fino): dwarf plants to 1 foot (0.3 m), small leaves, compact shape great for edging beds, flavor great for pesto
Genovese: tall, slow to bolt, large dark green leaves, intense spicy basil fragrance; 'Genovese Compact' is about half as tall and good for small gardens or containers
Lettuce Leaf (O. *basilicum* var. *crispum*): 85 days, very productive, large crinkled leaves
Mammoth (Mostruoso): very large leaves, sweet and spicy, similar to lettuce-leafed basil but not as crinkly and has larger leaves

HOW TO PREPARE: The aromatic leaves of basil are used fresh in soups, salads (including *panzanella*, a rustic salad made with slightly stale bread and vegetables), bruschetta, and pesto. It is sometimes tucked in sandwiches instead of lettuce. In Italy basil flavors minestrone, sandwiches, marinara, zucchini frittata, and fresh and marinated mozzarella.

BEANS

(*fagioli rampicanti*: pole beans; *fagioli nani*: bush beans; *fagiolini*: snap beans) *Phaseolus vulgaris*

FAVA BEANS

(*fave*) *Vicia faba*

Beans are beloved in Italy. Italians use the standard cylindrical green beans, but they also favor broad, flat green and yellow beans called romano beans and the coiled ones called anellino beans. These beans seem to have a richer flavor than most green-bean varieties and are worth seeking out. Shelled beans are also widely grown in Italy, particularly the white kidney-shaped cannellini and the lovely red-speckled borlotto. Use them fresh or dried.

Ancient Romans relied on the broad fava beans as one of their staples. In Italy the special sweetness of these beans is prized, particularly when they are harvested very young. Favas are still very flavorful when fully mature, but their skins must be peeled off before preparation—and this is a real labor of love.

HOW TO GROW: Beans are grown as annuals and do well in most climates. Plant snap and shelling beans after all danger of frost is past; the purple and wax varieties can tolerate colder soil than the green snap bean. All beans need full sun and a good, loose garden loam with plenty of added humus. Sow seeds of bush beans 1 inch (2.5 cm) deep in rows 18 inches (46 cm) apart. Thin seedlings to 2 inches (5 cm) apart. Pole beans need a fairly strong trellis to climb on. Plant the seeds 1 inch (2.5 cm) deep, 6 inches (15 cm) apart. If the plants look pale midseason, fertilize them with fish emulsion. They are best watered deeply and infrequently; water at the base of the plants to prevent mildew.

Fava beans need a long, cool growing period of about 90 days and can even take repeated frost. In areas where winters don't dip below the low teens, plant favas in the fall. In very cold winter areas, plant favas at the same time as peas if you have long springs. Plant the seeds 2 inches (5 cm) deep, about 2–3 inches (5–8 cm) apart, in rows about 1½ feet (0.46 m) apart. Support the tall varieties

LEFT AND INSET: Fava beans

LEFT TO RIGHT: Yellow Anellino, Borlotto and Romano beans

with stakes and strings surrounding the outside of the beds.

In some areas bean beetles can be a serious problem. Other pests include beanloopers, whiteflies, aphids, and cucumber beetles. To help prevent diseases like anthracnose and leaf spots, plant resistant varieties, use drip irrigation rather than overhead watering, and do not work with the plants when they are wet. Black aphids are about the only pest of fava beans, and can be readily controlled by sprays of water.

Harvest snap beans when the seeds inside are still very small and the pods are tender. Harvest fresh shelling beans when the pods fill out noticeably but before they get dry. If the pods get too mature, allow them to dry for winter use. Young fava bean foliage can be harvested and cooked as you would other greens. The pods of the fava bean can be cooked when they're 3–4 inches (8–10 cm) long. Harvest young, tender fava beans that do not need their skins removed when they first start to fill out the pods. Or let the fava beans mature and use them fresh or dried.

VARIETIES

Anellino Beans (cornetti)

Green Anellino (Gancetto Verde): 85 days, pole, green Italian heirloom snap bean, stringless, crescent-shaped pod with rich bean flavor
Yellow Anellino (Gancetto Burro): 80 days, pole, yellow Italian heirloom snap bean, small, crescent-shaped pod, rich bean flavor

Fava Beans

Sweet Lorane: 240 days if sown in fall; small-seeded fava, good flavor, cold-hardy
Windsor: 75–80 days, bush, grows on an erect 2- to 4-foot (0.6–1.2 m) stalk, long green pods (up to 10 inches/25 cm), large, broad, light green beans

Purple Snap Beans

Trionfo Violetto: 60 days, pole, stringless, purple Italian heirloom, vigorous and attractive vines with deep lavender flowers

Romano Beans

Burro d'Ingegnoli (A cornetto largo giallo Burro

Cannellini

CAUTION Some males of Mediterranean descent are allergic to favas and should be wary when trying them for the first time.

d'Ingegnoli): 78 days, pole, stringless, very broad, deep yellow with large round seeds; very tender and almost buttery in flavor

Garafal Oro: 67 days, pole, large (up to 1 foot/0.3 m) beans with good flavor and delicate texture, very fast growing, vigorous vines, disease-resistant

Roma II: 50 days, bush, stringless, green, wide, thick pods with rich flavor, productive, resistant to bean mosaic virus

Wax Romano: 58 days, bush, light yellow, flavorful pods with meaty texture; vigorous plants

Shelling Beans

Cannellini: 75–80 days (for shelling, longer to dry), white, kidney-shaped, classic for Italian minestrone soup, also great for baking

Borlotto: 73 days, bush, Italian heirloom, colorful rose and cream pods, delicious creamy white beans with rosy speckles, sometimes referred to as cranberry beans

HOW TO PREPARE: In Italy standard green snap beans are usually boiled in a large pot or steamed until just tender. For salads they are left to cool; but most often they are cooked again, usually warmed in a sauté pan with olive oil (occasionally butter). Sometimes Parmesan cheese, anchovies, or garlic is added. Snap beans are served with pasta, sometimes combined with new potatoes or tomatoes. My favorite is snap beans with a pesto sauce served over penne pasta. The romano beans, particularly the yellow ones, must be watched carefully during cooking, as they turn to mush very quickly.

Fresh shelling beans like the borlotto types are usually boiled until just tender, then served with olive oil, Parmesan cheese, and garlic or used cold in a bean salad. They also are combined with leafy cutting types of chicory or broccoli raab and served in a sauce over pasta.

Fava beans in Italy are eaten at different stages. Young pods under 4 inches (10 cm) are boiled whole in salted water and seasoned with olive oil and garlic. When pods start to fill out, the small beans inside are sometimes served raw with salt or pecorino cheese at the end of a meal. Fava beans are most often cooked like lima beans, served with olive oil or butter and Parmesan cheese or cooked with pancetta. Simmer the young ones and add them to chopped tomatoes for a pasta sauce; use the older beans peeled or dried in hearty soups or with meats.

Dried beans are most popular in Italy, both the cannellini and the borlotto. Particularly in Tuscany and Florence there are numerous local dishes. White beans baked with olive oil, garlic, and sage is a favorite, as is the "twice boiled" soup *ribollita*. In *ribollita* the beans are simmered with aromatic vegetables until the soup is fairly thick; half the beans are then pureed and added back to the soup, which is eaten the next day. The soup is warmed, seasoned, and served over toasted bread. Tuscan black kale (*lacinato*) is the traditional vegetable added to this soup. Fresh or dried borlotto beans are integral to a mussel soup flavored with basil. Dried beans are important in the soup *pasta e fagioli*; they are also served with tuna over pasta or combined with rice and vegetables.

BORAGE
(borragine) Borago officinalis

This potherb is native to Europe and Africa and has a slight cucumber flavor. It's one of many spring greens gathered from the fields and hillsides of Italy to be used for salads and as a cooked green.

HOW TO GROW: Borage is an easily grown summer annual that sometimes acts like a biennial. Borage plants grow to about 2 feet (0.6 m) and have hairy gray leaves and deep blue, ½-inch (13 mm) star-shaped flowers. Plants are easily started from seeds. Sow the seeds in spring after all threat of frost is over, in average soil and full sun. You can harvest young leaves once the plants are established, and flowers anytime they appear. Borage often reseeds itself and winters over in mild climates.

Borage

> **CAUTION** Pregnant and lactating women should avoid borage flowers, as eating more than eight to ten flowers can cause milk to flow!

HOW TO PREPARE: In Italy very young leaves are added to salads and soups. The 1-inch (2.5 cm) borage flowers can be used in salads or to garnish drinks. The more mature leaves are hairy and are best consumed cooked, since cooking removes the hairy texture. Combine the leaves with other greens, both domestic and wild, in calzone and ravioli, in risotto, and on pizzas, or make them into nests that can be filled with eggs or cheese.

BROCCOLI, HEADING
(cavoli broccoli) Brassica oleracea var. *botrytis*

BROCCOLI, SPROUTING
(cavoli broccoli) B. oleracea var. *italica*

BROCCOLI RAAB
(cime di rapa, broccoletto di rapa, sparachetti) B. rapa (B. campestris)

CAULIFLOWER
(cavolfiore) B. oleracea var. *botrytis*

In addition to the familiar green heading broccolis, Italians grow sprouting broccolis that produce numerous small heads over a long season. Purple and white varieties of both the heading and sprouting broccolis, and the chartreuse, sculptured romanesco are also popular. While Americans categorize romanesco as broccoli, Italians consider it cauliflower. There are two more Italian "broccolis" to discuss—broccoli raab and *broccolo spigariello*. Broccoli raab is actually the flower shoot of a type of turnip and has slightly bitter green leaves. *Broccolo spigariello* is most probably a primitive cabbage and has dark green leaves with a grayish cast and grows as a very open broccoli plant with narrow heads. A broccoli relative, cauliflower, is very popular in Italy, and both white and purple types are grown.

HOW TO GROW: Standard broccoli is an annual, while cauliflower is actually a biennial. Both prefer cool weather and bolt (go to flower) in extremely hot weather. They are planted in very early spring

LEFT TO RIGHT: 'Romanesco' broccoli; Broccoli raab; Broccoli Calabrese; Purple sprouting broccoli

for summer bearing, or in summer or fall for winter bearing. In mild climates overwintering varieties can be planted. Both need full sun, with light shade in hot climates. Start broccoli seeds indoors six weeks before your last average frost date. Plant cauliflower a little earlier, as it grows more slowly. Plant seeds ½ inch (13 mm) deep. Or buy transplants and place them in rich soil about two weeks before the last average frost date. Plants should be spaced 1½ feet (0.46 m) apart, or 2½ feet (0.76 m) for the romanesco varieties. Broccoli and cauliflower are heavy feeders and need a consistent supply of water and nutrients, especially nitrogen. Work compost and blood meal or a balanced organic fertilizer into the soil before planting and again three or four weeks after planting. Mulching helps retain the necessary moisture.

Broccoli and cauliflower tend to be more vigorous and have fewer pest and disease problems than do cabbages. Flea beetles, imported cabbageworm, and cutworms may be problems. The maggot of the cabbage root fly is another possible pest. Use floating row covers to prevent the fly from laying her eggs or the larvae from entering the soil by placing a 12-inch (30 cm) square of tar paper or black plastic directly over the roots of the plant. Cut a slit about 6 inches long from one edge directly to the middle of the square and slip the square around the plant. Good garden hygiene is your best prevention against diseases.

Harvest broccoli when the buds begin to swell but before they open. Once the primary head is harvested, most broccoli varieties produce many smaller heads. Most cauliflower heads need protection from the sun. Modern varieties have leaves that grow over the head, but some heirlooms need to have the leaves tied up around the head. Harvest cauliflower heads at the base when they are very full but before the curds have begun to separate.

The less well known broccolis raab and *spigariello* are both annuals and are grown like sprouting broccolis; their seeds are sown in early spring.

Both grow to harvestable size quite quickly. The plants may be fall-planted in mild climates, with the shoots being harvested over the winter. Plant the seeds ¼–½ inch (6–13 mm) deep in rows 1½–2 feet (0.46–0.6 m) apart in full sun. Thin to 4–6 inches (10–15 cm) apart. Both can tolerate light frosts. Harvest the young leaves, stems, and flower buds just as the buds form a small head but before the flowers open.

VARIETIES
Broccoli
Calabrese: 58 days, Italian green sprouting broccoli with a long season of side shoots after the main head is cut

De Cicco: 48 days, traditional Italian heirloom with 3–4-inch (8–10 cm) main heads and a heavy yield of side shoots after the main head is cut, long cutting season, leaves used like collards after the plant is well established

Minaret: 75–85 days; earlier, smaller, and more uniform than 'Romanesco'

Paragon: 75 days, 8-inch (20 cm) heads, tender and sweet stems

Romanesco: 85 days; conical, chartreuse broccolis; slow grower; attractive conical whorl of mild, sweet florets; large plant; uneven quality heads

Cauliflower

Alverda: 80–100 days from fall planting, green-headed, uniform and productive, good for over-wintering in mild climates

Snow Crown: 50 days, hybrid white cauliflower, dependable production, good for early spring

Violet Queen: hybrid cauliflower with purple heads, one of the easiest cauliflowers to grow, space 12 inches (30 cm) apart, self-blanching

Unusual Broccoli

Broccolo Spigariello: loose-growing type of broccoli with very small heads, grows to 2½–3 feet (0.75–0.9 m), white flowers, produces over a long season if flower heads are harvested, available only from Pagano

Sessantina Grossa: 35 days, early, large buds, thick, tender stems

Spring Raab: 45 days, Italian heirloom, slow-bolting, late variety that can be wintered over in mild climates

HOW TO PREPARE: Broccolis are mostly associated with the southern parts of Italy. Usually the florets are cooked in boiling salted water until just tender and then reheated with olive oil and seasonings. Another presentation is to simmer the broccoli in white wine, olive oil, and garlic. The sprouting and romanesco types of broccoli cook more quickly than do the standard types. Small florets of both types can be marinated and used in antipasto or steamed and flavored with anchovies and garlic and served over fettucine. Broccoli florets are lovely in soup with small potatoes or baked with seasonings, bread crumbs, and cheese.

The slightly bitter flower shoots of broccoli raab are blanched or steamed and then served with olive oil and garlic. They can be seasoned and served over orechiette pasta or added to soups. In southern Italy broccoli raab is cooked with salt pork and garlic. *Broccolo spigariello* is sometimes called black soup broccoli and is most often used in soup as you would Tuscan black kale.

Cauliflower is very popular in Italy, especially in the north. The basic preparation is to boil it in salted water and then finish it with seasonings like olive oil, butter, garlic, fennel seeds, vinegar, or Parmesan cheese.

Cauliflower can be added to a frittata, breaded and fried, or sauced with a béchamel and baked with a little ham and seasonings. It can also be combined with tomatoes, seasonings, and pine nuts and served over pasta.

LEFT: Savoy cabbage
INSET: Tuscan black kale

CABBAGE, SMOOTH
(cavolo cappuccio) Brassica oleracea var. *capitata*

CABBAGE, SAVOY
(cavolo verza) B. oleracea var. *bulata*

TUSCAN BLACK KALE
(cavolo lacinato nero, black kale, dinosaur kale, lacinato kale*) B. oleracea* var. *acephala*

Italians use the puckery Savoy types of cabbage, with their handsome crinkled leaves, as well as the red and green ball-like smooth cabbages. Tuscan black kale is particularly favored in some areas of northern Italy.

HOW TO GROW: Cabbages are best grown as cool-season annuals and are usually started in early spring or midsummer, depending on the variety. They bolt and can get quite bitter-tasting in extremely hot weather. Most gardeners start Tuscan black kale in midsummer for a fall harvest. Transplant cabbages and kale into rich soil filled with organic matter. Both need full sun, or light shade in hot climates. Plant cabbage seeds 2–3 inches (5–8 cm) apart, ½ inch (13 mm) deep. Thin or transplant small varieties 12 inches (30 cm) apart and larger ones 24 inches (61 cm) apart. As cabbages tend to be top-heavy, when transplanting, place them lower in the soil than you would most vegetables—up to their first set of true leaves (the first leaves after the seed leaves). Plant kale seeds ½ inch (13 mm) deep, 1 inch (2.5 cm) apart, and thin to 12–18 inches (30–46 cm) apart. Cabbages and kales are heavy feeders, so add a balanced organic fertilizer: 1 US cup worked into the soil around each plant at planting time. They need regular and even watering and a substantial mulch.

Cabbages are susceptible to many pests and diseases; kale has fewer problems. See page 34 for information on cabbage family pests and diseases.

Harvest cabbages anytime after they have started to form a ball, but before they become so large that they split. Mature cabbages can take temperatures as low as 20ºF/-6.5ºC. If a hard freeze is expected, harvest all the cabbages and store them in a cool place. Start harvesting young leaves of Tuscan black kale when the plant has eight to ten leaves. Tuscan black kale is more tender than most kales and will not overwinter where the soil freezes.

VARIETIES
Cabbages
Dynamo: 70 days, 2½-pound (1.1 kg) green heads that resist splitting, plant in spring and again in fall, resistant to fusarium yellows
Green Glitter: 80 days, dark green 3½-pound (1.6 kg) heads, holds up well in the garden for winter harvest
Rougette: 80 days, deep red, 3-pound (1.4 kg) heads
Savoy Ace: 80 days, Savoy-type, good quality, up to 4½ pounds (2 kg), highly resistant to fusarium yellows and insect damage

Tuscan Black Kale

Lacinato: 62 days; Italian heirloom; unique, dark blue-green kale with thick crinkly leaves and a sweet flavor

HOW TO PREPARE: The Savoy cabbages are usually the mildest flavored and most popular in Italy, especially in the Milan area. Salads combining thinly sliced Savoy cabbage and red radicchios are gorgeous. Cabbages are often stuffed with meat or rice; and they are commonly used in minestrone soup.

Tuscan black kale is most often used in soups, especially in *ribollita*, a twice-cooked soup with white beans served over country-style bread. It is also featured in Tuscan black kale pesto. Other uses include adding it to a stew with pork, and cooking it with potatoes and serving it over penne. Red cabbage is cooked in the same manner as in much of Europe, poached in red wine.

CAPERS

(capperi) Capparis spinosa

Capers are shrubby tender perennials with edible flower buds.

HOW TO GROW: Capers are very susceptible to frost. They're grown in a greenhouse or outdoors in USDA Zones 9 through 11. Plant them in fast-draining soil, as they rot readily. The plants are evergreen and spread to about 5 feet (1.5 m) if not cut down by frost. Their green, round, fleshy leaves are carried on arching branches. Their lovely flowers have 2–3-inch (5–8 cm) petals and long pink stems. Obtain plants from a specialty mail-order nursery and set them out in a warm, sunny place as soon as there is no danger of frost. Look for a spineless variety. (If you must start plants from seed, freeze the seeds in sand for two weeks prior to germination. Germination rates are very low, so plant lots of extra seeds.) Water trans-

plants in and then keep the watering to a minimum. Fertilizer is not usually needed. Prune the plants occasionally to prevent them from becoming straggly. Capers grow very slowly.

When harvesting for pickling, pick flower buds just before they open. The buds should be left in the dark for a few hours before they are pickled.

HOW TO PREPARE: The flower buds are salted or pickled and used to add flavor to hors d'oeuvres, stuffings, sauces, vinaigrettes, and vegetable salads. Sprinkle them over pizzas and sliced tomatoes or add them to pasta sauces. To salt capers, first dry them in the sun; then layer them with rock salt. Before using, soak the salted capers for half an hour or so to remove the salt.

BELOW: Capers growing on an Italian hillside
INSET: A closeup of the caper flower

ARDOON

(....rdoi) Cynara cardunculus

....rdoon is a wild relative of the artichoke, but
....like the artichoke, its stalks, not its flower buds,
.... eaten.

HOW TO GROW: Sow seeds of cardoon in early
spring, inside in cold climates and outside in mild-
winter ones. Plant the seedlings or seeds in a trench
about 1 foot (0.3 m) deep in which the soil has
been well prepared with organic matter. Keep the
plants very well watered and fertilized to produce
vigorous growth, or the stalks get bitter and tough.
In the fall blanch the stalks to make them sweeter
and more tender (see page 20). For more general
information on climate considerations and cultural
requirements, see "Artichokes, Globe," page 26.

HOW TO PREPARE: Remove the tough outside
stalks and string as you would with celery stalks.
Cut the stalks into 3-inch (8 cm) pieces. To prevent discoloration and to cut some of the bitterness, preblanch them for 5–7 minutes in water to
which a couple of tablespoons of vinegar or lemon
juice has been added. Boil the stalks for 45 minutes
or steam them until tender. Serve the stalks with
olive oil or an herb or anchovy butter, or bake
them with butter or a béchamel sauce and serve
with Parmesan cheese. Or add them to a fritter, or
marinate them for a dramatic part of your antipasto presentation. When very young, cardoons are
eaten raw and used to accompany *bagna cauda*, a
hot garlic, anchovy sauce.

LEFT: Cardoon in bloom
ABOVE LEFT: Cut stalk
TOP: Cardoon plant

CHARD
(bieta, Swiss chard*) Beta vulgaris* var. *cicla*

Chard, a close cousin of the beet, is a mild-flavored green that tolerates a lot more heat than most. The chard favored by Italians has crunchy, large white midribs and deep green ruffled leaves.

HOW TO GROW: Start chard in early spring or late summer. Swiss chard grows upright and straight, even to 4 feet (1.2 m) tall when it bolts.

Plant chard seeds ¼–½ inch (6–13 mm) deep, 6 inches (15 cm) apart, and thin to 1 foot (0.3 m) apart. Plant in full sun and neutral soil with lots of added organic matter. For tender, succulent leaves, keep plants well watered. Mulch with a few inches of organic matter. When plants are about six weeks old, fertilize them with ½ US cup of balanced organic fertilizer for every 5 feet (1.5 m) of row. (Weight equivalent will vary depending on type used.)

A few pests and diseases bother chard, namely slugs and snails (especially when the plants are young), and leaf miners, a fly larvae.

To harvest chard, remove the outside leaves at the base; tender new leaves will keep coming throughout the season.

VARIETIES

Argentata: 55 days, Italian heirloom, large green-and-white chard, plants widely adapted and among the most cold tolerant

Paros: 55 days, a French green-and-white traditional-type chard with milder and more tender stalks than some domestic varieties

HOW TO PREPARE: Young chard leaves are tender and mild; they are a staple in many Italian recipes, often combined with or substituted for spinach. When chard leaves are large, the long, crisp ribs are removed from the greens. Blanch the leaves in boiling salted water, then drain them and squeeze out the excess water. They can then be warmed in a pan with olive oil and lemon juice, with or without garlic, or used in frittatas, soups, and risottos. Chard leaves are also used in ravioli stuffings, in barley soup with cannellini beans, and even in a dessert tart along with ricotta cheese.

In Italy the stems of Swiss chard are considered its best virtue. The strings in the stems are removed. Then the stems are boiled in salted water, drained, and served with olive oil and seasonings, folded over themselves and stuffed with meat and mushrooms, or sautéed in butter and finished with Parmesan cheese.

Chard

CHICORIES
(cicorie) Cichorium intybus

BELGIAN ENDIVE
(Witloof chicory)

ITALIAN WILD, CUTTING CHICORIES
(cicorie)

RADICCHIOS
(cicorino, radicchio, radicchieto)

Chicories are a cool-weather salad staple throughout most of Italy. They include the rustic cutting chicories sometimes found growing wild in Italy, the burgundy-colored heading radicchios, and the elegant Belgian endive. All chicories share a mildly bitter taste that can be mitigated by blanching them and soaking them in salted water. The variety and growing temperature are also factors in the level of bitterness.

HOW TO GROW: Generally chicories are easy to grow, though they prefer cool growing conditions and often perform poorly in very hot summer areas. Plant all chicory seeds ¼ inch (6 mm) deep in good soil filled with organic matter, in full sun. (Or start seeds inside and transplant them when they are a few inches tall.) Thin seedlings to 8 inches (20 cm) apart and keep them fairly moist. Chicories have few pests and disease problems. The challenges to producing most chicories is in the timing and the pre- and post-harvest treatment. And it's here that there are major differences by type.

Let's start with the easiest chicories to produce: the non-heading, leaf, cutting chicories. Some are categorized as Catalonian-type chicories in Italian catalogs. They are planted in early spring, or 60 days before the onset of cool fall weather. They can be harvested when young and mild by cutting the leaves with scissors when they are 3–4 inches (8–10 cm) tall. If the weather stays cool, they can be cut again a few weeks later.

The leaves of the cutting chicories are best if harvested when young. Leaf chicories can also be grown over the winter in most climates, with the new, tender growth harvested in the spring. One such chicory is grown for its twisted succulent stems as well as its leaves—'Puntarella.' To make it less bitter, garden blanch it by inverting a flowerpot over the plant a week or so before harvesting (see page 20).

In contrast, producing the beautiful ruby red and white radicchios and the silky chicons of Belgian endive is another matter. A little know-how and timing are needed. To produce the chicories Americans call radicchios, choosing the proper variety and planting time is the first step. If you are new to growing radicchios, choose the modern radicchios; they are much easier to grow in most climates, as they pretty reliably head up and self-blanch in the garden. (The heirloom varieties are generally climate-specific to Italy.) In cold climates plant the modern varieties in late spring; if they don't form round heads on their own, cut back the plants in early fall—usually they will resprout, form a head, and be ready for harvest four to six weeks later. In parts of the country where winters stay above 10°F/-12°C, plant radicchios in late spring for a fall crop or in the fall for a harvest in the spring. The red radicchios are a bit unnerving, as most young plants start out with loose green leaves in the garden, then round heads form, and the inner hearts turn red at maturity. At harvest time, remove the outer green wrapper-leaves to reveal a center that is a deep, dark wine color with white midribs.

Belgian endive is another story; it is always blanched. In cold climates, start seeds in early spring and dig up the plants after the first frost. In mild-climate areas start plants in summer and dig them up in early fall. The plants are then blanched (see page 20).

VARIETIES
Cutting, Non-Heading Chicories
Catalonian Dentarella: Catalonian-type chicory, has dandelion-like leaves and thick stems, can be planted in fall and will winter over for a spring

FROM LEFT TO RIGHT Radicchios in the garden and (far right) after harvest. **BELOW:** Cutting Chicory.

harvest in all but the coldest climates

Catalogna Frastagliata: 65 days, a Catalonian-type variety, looks like a large dandelion

Catalonian Puntarella: 120 days from fall planting, another Catalonian type with twisted stems, succulent variety used for spring salads, overwinters in most climates

Ceriolo (Grumulo): 120 days from fall planting, a green cutting chicory for spring harvest

Radicchios

Chioggia Red Precoce No. 1: 60 days, modern red round radicchio that is widely adapted

Firebird: 74 days in north, modern red round radicchio

Giulio: about 90 days, spring-planting type, modern red round radicchio

Medusa: 65 days, hybrid, modern red round, radicchio for spring or fall planting

Red Treviso: deep burgundy, long, open heads; considered the gold standard of radicchios; heirloom variety acclimatized to Italy; must be cut back and forced

Belgian Endive

Flash: 110 days, hybrid Belgian endive bred for forcing without sand or soil around the shoots

Witloof Zoom: new hybrid Belgian endive for forcing without sand or soil around the shoots

HOW TO PREPARE: All types of chicories are usually sliced or torn into bite-size pieces and eaten

raw in salads, combined with sliced fennel. The red radicchios can be added to a salad raw or after they have been braised, grilled, or roasted. Grilled radicchio can be added to pasta dishes, used as part of an antipasto, or served as a side dish.

To cut the bitterness of raw chicories, shred them fine, soak them in salted water for 1 hour, drain, and use a dressing with balsamic vinegar or add honey. The cutting chicories are used in salad when they're very young and are served as potherbs when they're more mature—usually parboiled, drained, and seasoned with olive oil and lemon juice, or sautéed with garlic. They are then used to top pizzas, in frittatas, or in risottos.

Belgian endive is most often used as a bed for, or in salads with, other vegetables, seafood, and meats. The individual leaves are removed from the chicon and placed on a platter, with other ingredients arranged on them, or they are braised whole in butter or olive oil and lemon juice.

Dandelion

DANDELION, COMMON
(dente di leone, radichella) Taraxacum officinale

Dandelion greens are flavorful and add a slightly bitter richness to a salad, as well as lots of nutrition. Grow your own dandelions or gather them from wild areas early in the spring.

HOW TO GROW: Dandelions prefer full sun and slightly acidic soil. Plant these perennials as seeds ½ inch (13 mm) deep directly in the soil in the spring or fall, in rich, fertile loam, and keep them fairly moist. Thin seedlings to 8 inches (20 cm) apart and mulch to control weeds. Dandelions have very few pest and disease problems. Start harvesting after about three months. Harvest only the youngest, tender leaves. For the most delicate flavor, blanch the leaves by tying them up at the top as you would escarole. Do not let dandelions go to seed, or they will become a nuisance.

VARIETIES
Pissenlit: 92 days, notched leaves usually blanched
Thick-Leaved Improved: 95 days, large leaves good as a potherb, blanched leaves good in salads

HOW TO PREPARE: When harvested very young and garden-blanched, dandelions can be used in large amounts; if strong-flavored, they should be used sparingly or soaked in cold salted water for a few hours. Dandelion greens are eaten raw in salads dressed with olive oil, salt, and vinegar or lemon juice. In Emelia dandelions are dressed with warm bits of pancetta. Dandelions are also served as a pot herb in rissotto, frittatas, and soups.

EGGPLANT
(melanzana) Solanum melongena var. *esulentum*

Eggplant, which is very popular in Italy, is a tender, herbaceous perennial that's usually grown as an annual.

HOW TO GROW: Eggplants are so susceptible to freezing that it is best to start seeds indoors six to eight weeks before the average date of your last frost. The seeds germinate best at 80°F/26.7°C. Plant the seeds ¼ inch (6 mm) deep, in flats or peat pots. Eggplant takes about a week to germinate in a warm room. When all danger of frost is past and the soil has warmed up, place the plants in the garden 24 inches (61 cm) apart and water them well. Grow eggplant in full sun in rich, well-drained garden loam that is fertilized with blood meal and manure. Mulch with organic matter to retain both heat and moisture. If you are growing eggplant in a cool climate, cover the soil with black plastic to retain heat. To increase the yield and

to keep the plants healthy, feed them about three times during the growing season with fish emulsion and liquid kelp. Eggplant needs moderate watering and should never be allowed to dry out.

Flea beetles, spider mites, and whiteflies can be a problem. Flea beetles often appear early in the season, right after transplanting. Spider mites can be a nuisance in warm, dry weather. Nematodes are sometimes a problem in the South. Verticillium wilt and phomopsis blight are common disease problems in humid climates.

Eggplant is ready to harvest when it is full colored but has not yet begun to lose any of its sheen. Plants produce more fruit when they are harvested regularly.

VARIETIES

Italian varieties of eggplants vary in size and color. The most common are purple and elongated, but lavender and white varieties and round and cylindrical ones are grown as well.

Bambino: 75 days, hybrid, round, deep purple, small fruit good for pickling and stuffing

Italian White (Bianco Ovale): 75 days, 3–4-inch (8–10 cm) roundish white fruit, milder than purple varieties

Listada de Gandia: 75 days, striking white with purple stripes fruit, thin skins, not recommended for northern gardens

Rosa Bianca: 75 days, spectacular, productive, bright lavender fruits that are creamy, mild-flavored, and of high-quality

Violetta di Firenz: 60 to 80 days, spectacular lavender eggplant from Italy, large fruits sometimes with wide white stripes

Violetta Lunga: 8 inches (20 cm) long, deep purple, just right for slicing

Vittoria: 61 days, hybrid, long slender Italian type for slicing

HOW TO PREPARE: Italians salt eggplants and let some of the water drain out before using them in some recipes, especially if they are to be fried. Eggplant absorbs flavors well and may be browned by sautéing or grilling. Italians serve it with Parmesan cheese or tomato sauce, in lasagna, and with roasted garlic. Other Italian dishes include eggplant caviar, which is a term used to describe roasted or grilled eggplant that has been combined with garlic and seasonings and mashed. Deep-fried eggplant is served as a side dish, either plain or sauced. Italian dishes call for stuffing eggplants with herbs and anchovies or bread and mushrooms. Grilled eggplant is served with pesto or nepitalla butter, garnished with chopped arugula or basil, or added to a pasta or polenta dish with other vegetables and given a marinara sauce. And then there is the most famous Italian eggplant dish—eggplant parmigiana—in which eggplant is deep-fried and dressed with tomatoes and cheeses.

INSET: Eggplant.
LEFT: Listada de Gandia; Violetta Lunga; Rosa Bianca and 'White Sword' eggplants

FENNEL, FLORENCE

(*finocchio*, bulbing fennel) *Foeniculum vulgare dulce*

FENNEL, WILD

(*finocchio selvatico*, leaf fennel, herb fennel)
  F. vulgare

Florence bulbing fennel is a favorite Italian vegetable and is often included in antipasto dishes and salads. This ferny-topped plant, about 2 feet (0.6 m) tall, looks a little like a swollen white celery. It is easy to grow and generally requires cool weather. Wild fennel is used as an herb for the anise flavor its leaves and seeds impart to salads and cooked dishes.

HOW TO GROW: Though a perennial, wild fennel, with its beautiful, ferny foliage, is usually grown as an annual. Start wild fennel in the spring from seeds or transplants after the weather has warmed up. One or two plants are enough for the average family. Plant them in full sun in well-drained, fertile soil. These ferny plants grow to 3 feet/0.9 m (so give them room to spread) and produce flat sprays of yellow flowers. Keep fennel moist until it is well established; after that, be careful not to overwater. Harvest the leaves as soon as the plants get 4–5 inches (10–13 cm) tall. Dry the brown seeds in a paper bag in a warm, dry place. Store the dried seeds in a glass jar. Cut back the plants in spring to keep them looking trim. Keep the seed heads removed, as fennel reseeds and can become a weed.

Florence bulbing fennel grows to perfection only in cool weather. Therefore, in cold climates Florence fennel is started as soon as the soil can be worked in the spring, or planted in summer for a fall harvest. In areas where winters seldom dip below 28°F/-2.2°C, it can be grown as either a fall or a spring crop. As a rule, fall-planted crops are the most rewarding. Grow Florence fennel in full sun in fertile, well-drained soil. Thin plants to 6–8 inches (15–20 cm) apart. In short-season areas harvest the plants as baby vegetables, only 2 inches (5 cm) across, instead of trying to grow large bulbs, which require a long, cool season. If

Fennel

you have the needed long season, harvest the bulb when it is 3–5 inches (8–13 cm) across by cutting the bulbing stem off at ground level with a knife. If conditions are suitable, "baby" fennels will sprout from the crown.

VARIETIES

Fennel, Leaf: 60 days, herb fennel, green feathery leaves, slow-bolting, to about 3 feet (0.9 m)
Zefa Fino: 80 days, bulbing, Florence fennel, bolt-resistant, large bulbs

HOW TO PREPARE: Use the slightly anise-flavored bulbs as you would celery; or braise fennel, drizzle it with olive oil, and sprinkle it with anchovy bits or Parmesan cheese. The most common fennel presentation in Italy is to cut it into wedges and serve it with *pinzimonio*, a simple dipping sauce made of the best olive oil and salt. Fennel is often served as part of an antipasto, sometimes sliced paper thin, or in a salad with arugula or oranges.

The leaves of the leaf or wild fennel can be used to flavor salads, sauces, fish, soups, stews, salad dressings, and pasta. Throw the dry plant prunings onto the grill when you are preparing fish for a great, rich flavor. Use the seeds in soups and in seafood sauces. In parts of Italy wild fennel pollen is gathered and used to flavor pork and chicken dishes.

LETTUCE
(lattuga) Lactuca sativa

Lettuce is native to the Italian peninsula and the Italians enjoy many varieties.

HOW TO GROW: Lettuce is a cool-season annual crop that can be grown in temperate gardens worldwide. Most varieties go to seed or become bitter rapidly once hot weather arrives. In warm weather lettuce grows better with afternoon or filtered shade. In mild-winter areas lettuce grows through the winter.

Lettuce prefers soil high in organic matter. It needs regular moisture and profits from light feedings of fish emulsion or fish meal fertilizer every few weeks. Sow seeds ⅛ inch (3 mm) deep outdoors, start indoors in flats, or buy transplants. You can start lettuce outside as soon as you can work the soil in spring. Plant seeds 2 inches (5 cm) apart and ⅛ inch (3 mm) deep. Keep seed beds uniformly moist until the seedlings appear. Thin seedlings to between 6 and 12 inches (15 and 30 cm) apart, depending on the variety. Failure to thin seedlings can result in disease problems.

Protect seedlings from birds, slugs, snails, and aphids until they get fairly good sized by using floating row covers and by hand picking. Botrytis, a gray mold fungus disease, can cause the plants to rot off at the base. Downy mildew, another fungus, causes older leaves to get whitish patches that eventually die.

You can harvest lettuce at any stage. If possible, harvest during the cool of the day. Leaf lettuces can be harvested one leaf at a time or in their entirety. Heading lettuces are generally harvested by cutting off the head at the soil line.

VARIETIES
Biondo Liscio: tender, small-leafed lettuce perfect for *misticanza* and cut-and-come-again harvesting
Lollo Biondo: pale green version of 'Lollo Rossa,' heat-resistant
Lollo Rossa: 56 days, Italian variety, looseleaf, distinctive, frilly leaves, red margins, pale green heart, good for cut-and-come-again plantings
Marvel of Four Seasons (Four Seasons): 60 days; known in Italy as 'Meraviglia di Quattro Stagioni,' striking, bright red outer leaves, pale pink-and-cream interior, tender yet crisp
Red Perella (Perella Red): 52 days, beautiful Italian variety of baby lettuce, 6–7-inch (15–18 cm) rosettes of green leaves shading to rich red
Resisto: an Italian crisp-head lettuce that can be sown in summer and is resistant to bolting and to most lettuce diseases
Rossa d'America: Italian looseleaf lettuce, pale green leaves tipped with rosy red, harvest at 4 inches (10 cm) for cut-and-come-again crop
Verde d'Inverno: Italian romaine-type lettuce for fall sowing, resistant to frost, medium green leaves with prominent ribs

HOW TO PREPARE: Lettuces are used in Italian salads, which are generally a mixture of many different types of greens with complementary flavors—some tangy, some bitter, and some sweet—that change with the seasons. Salads are often dressed simply with olive oil and vinegar or lemon juice. Lettuce is occasionally cooked in soups and is stuffed with meats of all types, fish, and vegetables and herbs.

Lettuce

NEPITELLA
(nepitella) Calamintha nepeta

This mellow mint has been used by generations of Italians to flavor mushrooms and many vegetables.

HOW TO GROW: Nepitella is a low-growing perennial herb that is easily grown in USDA Zones 5 to 10. It grows to about a foot (0.3 m) and has small gray-green leaves and sprays of tiny lavender to white flowers. Obtain plants from specialty herb nurseries and set them out in fast-draining soil. Give them afternoon shade in hot climates and moderate watering in arid areas. Cut back plants after flowering and apply a balanced organic fertilizer. In mild climates a second pruning may be needed to keep the plant trim and in bounds. Nepitella reseeds itself and occasionally becomes a weed. In cold-winter areas mulch nepitella in the fall to protect it against frosts.

HOW TO PREPARE: Nepitella tastes like a mellow mint with a bit of oregano. Called *mentuccia* in certain dialects, this herb grows wild in parts of Italy. It is used in stuffed artichokes and with eggplant, potatoes, zucchini, and grilled fish; in some parts of the country it is considered essential in some mushroom dishes.

> **CAUTION** Large amounts of certain calamints have been known to cause miscarriages; to be safe, pregnant women should avoid all calamints.

Nepitella

ONIONS

BULBING ONIONS
(cipolle) Allium cepa

GARLIC
(aglio) A. sativum

ROCAMBOLE
(serpent garlic, Italian garlic)
A. sativum var. *ophioscorodon*

HOW TO GROW: Onions, garlic, and rocambole are all members of the genus *Allium*. Plants in this group prefer cool weather, particularly in their juvenile stages, and soil rich in organic matter and phosphorus. They are heavy feeders and should be fertilized, as well as watered, throughout the growing season.

Bulbing Onions

Bulbing onions are grown from seeds or from young bulbs, called sets. As biennials, onions bulb up the first year when grown from seed and flower the second if they're replanted. When grown from sets, they usually both bulb and flower the first year.

It is important to select the right variety of onion for your climate and time of year because the bulbs are formed according to length of day. There are short-day, medium-day, and long-day onion varieties. Short-day onions are most successful when spring-planted in southern regions of the country.

Long-day onions are ideal for northern areas with their long summer days. Medium-day onions do well in most parts of the country.

The bulbing season can be prolonged by planting seeds indoors six to eight weeks before you can safely plant them outdoors. Outside, sow onion seeds ¼ inch (6 mm) deep in the spring or put out sets; seeds or sets may be started in the fall or winter in mild climates. Many gardeners interplant onions among other vegetables and flowers, a practice that deters the onion maggot. Plant onions in rich, well-drained soil, and keep the soil moisture even during the growing season. Fertilize with a balanced organic fertilizer when plants are about 6 inches (15 cm) tall and beginning to bulb. Keep weeds and cultivation to a minimum, as onions are shallow rooted. Onions should be thinned to give each plant adequate room for unhampered development. Use the thinnings as scallions.

The most common pests of onions are the brown fly larvae, known as the onion maggot, and thrips. To cut down on infestations, practice crop rotation. Interplant onions with other plants so the pests can't easily crawl from onion to onion. With severe infestations, apply row covers and/or satu-

ABOVE: 'Italian Torpedo,' 'Rossa di Milano,' 'Giallo di Milano,' and small white onions
INSET: Growing onions

rate the soil with beneficial nematodes at planting time. Thrips are attracted to stressed onion plants, especially those that are moisture-stressed. Place light blue sticky traps to attract adult thrips and treat the plants with insecticidal soap.

Onions may be harvested at any stage of development, though most people wait until the bulbs are fairly large. Onions for storage should not be harvested until their tops die down. You can hasten this process by bending the tops over. Then dig up the onions and let them stay on top of the soil to dry out for at least a day. The bulbs must be protected from sunburn, which you can do easily by covering them with their tops. Place the bulbs on a screen or hang them where there is good air circulation to "cure" (allow the skins to dry) for several additional weeks before their final storage. Storage varieties can be stored for three to four months.

VARIETIES

Most modern onion breeding has been for sweet onions, but the sharp, less sweet varieties are better for sauces, soups, and many long-cooking dishes. Lockhart Seeds (www.lockhartseeds.com) has a large selection of onions.

Bianca di Maggio: 80 days, flat, white, mid-size onion with mild flavor for a summer crop
Giallo di Milano ('Gialla Ramata di Milano'): 110 days, long-day, yellow, good storage
Italian Torpedo: 110 days, medium-day, Italian heirloom bottle onion, red, 4–6 inches (10–15 cm) long, 2–3 inches (5–8 cm) wide, does not store well
Red Burgermaster: 110 days, long-day, large red, sweet slicing onion, stores well
Rossa di Milano (Rossa Ramata di Milano): 110 days, long-day, Italian red, barrel-shaped, stores well, pungent flavor

Garlic

Walla Walla Sweet: 125 days if spring-seeded, 300 days if sown in late summer and left to over-winter; long-day; large, round onion, known for sweet and juicy flesh; best if seeded in time to overwinter

Garlic

Garlic plants are grown from cloves that can be purchased in heads from nurseries or food markets. Although easily grown, garlic performs best in milder, dry climates. It should be planted in the fall or early spring. Ample and consistent water is needed for the first four or five months of development, as is full sun.

Divide the heads into individual cloves and plant them about 1 inch (2.5 cm) deep and 4 inches (10 cm) apart. Garlic does best in soil with a good deal of added organic matter. In areas of extremely cold winters, mulch with straw to protect fall-started plants. Garlic is hardy to all but the most severe cold and is virtually free of pests and diseases. Garlic greens may be lightly harvested and used in cooking as you would scallions, in both fall and late spring, as long as the plants are not depleted. Garlic is ready for harvest when the plant tops turn brown and die back. Dig the heads carefully and allow them to dry on a screen in the shade, protected from sunburn. To prevent rotting and so that you can braid them, retain several inches of dried stalk on each head. Store garlic in a cool, dry area with good air circulation.

VARIETIES

Overall, smaller types are considered to have the best flavor. Filaree Garlic Farm (www.filareefarm. com) specializes in organically grown garlic.
Early Red Italian: early maturing, medium to large bulbs splotched with red, cloves milk white
German Extra-Hardy: very winter-hardy, good for northern gardens, good flavor, keeps well
Gilroy California Late: good flavor, long-keeping, juicy cloves, ideal for garlic braiding
Italian Late: late season, softneck, pungent, stores and braids well

Rocambole

Rocambole is a rich-flavored type of garlic with large, easily peeled cloves. Also known as Italian garlic, hardneck garlic, or serpent garlic—the latter for the shape of its stem—it is a top-setting garlic that forms bulbils (small bulbs) at the top of the stem. Either these or the cloves formed underground may be used in any recipe calling for garlic, or they can be planted to continue the crop.

VARIETIES

Hillside: winter-hardy, hardneck type with small, strong-flavored cloves
Spanish Roja: midseason, hardneck type, a Northwest heirloom with true garlic flavor, does not do well in mild-winter areas

HOW TO PREPARE: Use strong, "hot" onions for rich onion flavor in dishes calling for long cooking or caramelizing. Use the mild onions for raw dishes.

The onion is the basis for many Italian dishes. It is used in *soffritto*, a mixture of onion, garlic, carrots, celery, herbs (especially parsley), and sometimes a slice of pancetta that is the starting point for many meat and vegetable dishes. Sweet red onions are used raw in salads. Onions can also stand on their own, baked with olive oil and balsamic vinegar, say, or stewed in butter and a meat stock. Anna Del Conte speaks of northern Italians roasting onions with the skins still on. When they are cooked through, they are peeled, sliced, and eaten with olive oil and salt. Other Italian favorites are onions in a frittata with potatoes and rosemary, ravioli stuffed with a potato dough with onions and peppermint, and tiny onions in a sweet and sour sauce.

Garlic is used as a flavoring in many Italian dishes, from marinated olives to most pasta sauces. Two classic dishes feature garlic: *agliata*, a sauce made of garlic, bread crumbs, and olive oil and served on mushrooms or grilled vegetables; and *bagna cauda*, or farmer's lunch, a sauce made with cream, anchovies, and garlic and served with vegetables and bread for dipping.

You can rub garlic on toasted bread and drizzle it with olive oil for an antipasto, put it on pizzas, use it in salad dressings, soups, stews and to flavor sautéed vegetables.

Whole heads can be roasted in the oven. Cut papery tops off the head, place the head on a baking sheet, drizzle with olive oil, and bake it at 400ºF/200ºC for about 20 minutes or until tender. Squeeze flesh out of cloves and spread on bread or use in dressings and vegetable dishes.

OREGANO AND SWEET MARJORAM
(origano) Origanum spp.

The European oreganos are scrubby perennials native to the arid mountainsides of the eastern Mediterranean, they have long been associated with Italy.

HOW TO GROW: Common (*Origanum vulgare*) and Greek oregano (*O. v.* sub. *hirtum*; synonym: *O. v. heracleoticum*) are hardy to USDA Zone 5. Oreganos do poorly under hot, humid conditions and are treated as summer annuals in areas where temperatures are regularly in the high eighties and above. Sweet marjoram (*O. marjorana*) can't withstand hard frosts and is often grown as a summer annual. Both must be planted in full sun in light, fast-draining soil. To ensure the best flavor, start plants from transplants or cuttings, not seeds. Cut back plants in late spring to encourage new growth, and again in midsummer to prevent them from becoming woody.

Greek oregano is considered by many to be the most flavorful European oregano. Before buying your oregano, taste it and see if it has a pleasant, spicy taste. The same holds true with marjoram.

HOW TO PREPARE: The oreganos are most associated with southern Italy and can be used in soups, marinara, pizza, salads, cooked vegetables, and most fish and meat dishes. Use them in marinades for olives and tomatoes.

PARSLEY
(prezzemolo) Petroselinum crispum

There are two major types of parsley—the curly one and the tall, flat-leafed type, rightly called Italian parsley.

   HOW TO GROW: Parsleys are biennials generally treated as annuals. The curly types have dark green, curly, finely divided leaves. They seldom grow more than a foot (0.3 m) tall. Flat-leaf or Italian parsley grows to 2 feet (0.6 m) and is a somewhat rangy plant. It's the preferred culinary parsley for flavoring in Italy because of its deep flavor and sweetness. Start seeds in the spring or buy plants from nurseries and set them out. The plants do best in full sun and in rich, organic soil high in organic matter. Fertilize parsley midseason with nitrogen.

INSETS, TOP: 'Greek' oregano
BOTTOM: Flat-leaf parsley

VARIETIES
Curly-leafed Parsley
Frisca Curly: 75 days, vigorous, extra-curly, sweet flavor without metallic overtones, mildew-resistant

Flat-leafed Parsley
Catalogno (Gigante Catalogno): 75 days, large leaves, good strong flavor
Gigante d'Italia (Giant Italian): 85 days, 2–3 feet, (0.6–0.9m) vigorous growth, rich flavor

   HOW TO PREPARE: Parsley is best used fresh, though it retains some flavor when frozen. The Italians most commonly use the flat-leaf parsley, primarily in cooked dishes. Curly parsley is primarily used for garnishing.
   Parsley is critical in Italian cooking. *Soffritto*, a mixture of onions, garlic, carrots, celery, and lots of parsley, is the basis for sauces, soups, stews, and fritattas. *Gremolata* is another flavoring mixture made with parsley, lemon peel, garlic, and olive oil.

SHELLING PEAS

(*piselli,* garden peas, green peas) *Pisum sativum*

Peas are most associated with northern Italy.

HOW TO GROW: Pea plants are either short bushes or long climbing vines from 6 feet (1.8 m) tall. Peas are annuals requiring well-prepared, humus-rich soil, full sun, high humidity, and cool weather. They can tolerate some frost but do poorly in hot weather. The soil should be neutral or slightly alkaline and well drained. Pea seeds should be planted directly into the garden in early spring. Plant seeds 1 inch (2.5 cm) deep and 4 inches (10 cm) apart in double rows—12-inch (30 cm) spacing between rows is sufficient. Sets of double rows can be planted 24 inches (61 cm) apart. Most pea varieties profit from a trellis. Supports should be placed in the ground at the time of planting. Peas need only a light fertilizing when about 6 inches (15 cm) tall but profit from regular and deep watering—1 inch (2.5 cm) per week is ideal. They also respond well to organic mulches.

Peas are most attractive to slugs, snails, and birds. Cover the seedlings until they are 6 inches (15 cm) high. Another pest, the pea weevil, is not usually a serious problem, but large numbers should be controlled. To deter them, try lightly dusting wet or dew-covered foliage with lime. Pea moths can be controlled with Bacillus thuringiensis. To prevent mildew, avoid afternoon overhead watering.

Ideally, peas should be harvested every day during the mature-pod stage. If left past maturity, they begin to lose their sweetness and become tough, and production declines. Shelling peas are ripe when the pods are filled out but before they begin to lose their glossy green color and start to harden.

VARIETIES

Lincoln: great-tasting heirloom pea; not as disease-resistant as some of the new varieties

Knight: 56 days, 1½–2-foot (0.46–0.6 m) vines, productive, 3½–4½-inch (9–11 cm) pods with sweet, medium-sized peas

Novella (Novella II): 57 days, semi-leafless variety, pronounced flowers and pods; neat and uniform bushy plants to 24 inches (61 cm) high.

HOW TO PREPARE: Standard peas are enjoyed as a side dish after being boiled briefly and then reheated in butter and seasonings. Peas are paired with prosciutto and served in a cream sauce over pasta; combined with rice and pancetta in a soup; or pureed and cooked to make a timballini, a molded creation made with eggs and seasonings. Fresh peas are also used in lovely spring soups in combination with other spring vegetables and herbs like sorrel, mint, and chives.

Shelling peas

PEPPERS

(peperoni, sweet peppers; *peperoncini,* hot peppers)
Capsicum spp.

Peppers are enjoyed most in southern Italy. Here they enjoy the large bells and the spicy Cayenne types.

HOW TO GROW: Peppers are a warm-weather crop. They cannot tolerate frost and won't set fruit unless the weather is at least 65°F/18.3°C but does not exceed 80°F/26.7°C. Start them in flats eight weeks before the average last frost date. When seedlings are about 4 inches (10 cm) tall and all danger of frost is past, transplant them. Do not move them out too early, as chilling them results in poor growth all season. Wait until night temperatures are above 55°F/12.8°C and the air and soil are warm and settled.

Plants should be placed at least 18 inches (46 cm) apart in full sun, or in partial shade in hot climates. They require deep, rich soil and regular watering and fertilizing. Peppers are heavy feeders and respond well to regular applications of manure, fish emulsion, and kelp. Should they develop paler than normal and curling leaves, try adding calcium in the form of dolomite.

Tender pepper plants can fall victim to snails, slugs, aphids, and cutworms. Otherwise, the plants are relatively pest-free. They are occasionally prone to the same diseases that afflict tomatoes. Keep plants mulched and the weeds under control.

Peppers continue to produce fruit until the weather cools. Sweet peppers come in a wide range of colors. Once sweet peppers get near full size, they can be picked at their green, red, or yellow stages. Hot peppers can also be picked at any color stage, but most are hotter if allowed to ripen fully.

VARIETIES
Sweet Peppers
Cherry Sweet (Sweet Cherry): 70 days, heirloom, green to red, sweet, cherry-shaped peppers, great for pickling and stuffing

Corno di Toro Giallo (Yellow Corno di Toro): 80–100 days, Italian pepper named for the shape, which is similar to a bull's horn; 6–12 inches (15–30 cm) long; sweet yellow flesh at maturity
Corno di Toro Rosso (Red Corno di Toro): 80–100 days, red version of the one above
Figaro: 68 days, sweet Italian heirloom pimiento, ripens to crimson red, great for roasting
Marconi : 70–80 days, Italian heirloom, large—up to 1 foot (0.3 m) long and 3 inches (8 cm) across at the shoulder—red or yellow sweet peppers
Peperoncini: 75 days, long thin sweet peppers for salad, pickled for antipasto, harvested when green and full size, turns red at maturity, shrubby 3-foot (0.9 m) plant, high-yielding
Quadrato d'Asti Giallo: 85 days, Italian, green to gold, blocky shape, sweet pepper

Hot Peppers
Cherry: 80 days, bright red hot pepper, round, good for pickling

Super Cayenne: 70 days, early, slim, 3–4-inch (8–10 cm) (long red peppers, high-yielding, 2-foot-tall (0.6 m) plant

HOW TO PREPARE: Sweet bell peppers are used raw in salads and antipasto, or roasted and marinated. They are braised with onions and tomatoes and served as a side dish called *peperonata*, used in sauces for pasta with anchovies or pancetta, and stuffed with bread crumbs, capers, anchovies, and olives or with pasta. In a few parts of southern Italy peppers are dried like tomatoes and used over the winter or made into a paste and spread on bread or used as a condiment. Grilled peppers are marinated with garlic, anchovies, and capers.

The spicier peppers are pickled or used to add a "kick" to soups, seafood, and stews, especially in the south. In Abruzzi hot peppers are used more than anywhere else in Italy, especially in pasta dishes.

FROM LEFT TO RIGHT:
Cherry peppers, bell peppers and 'Quadrato d'Asti Giallo'

SPINACH

(spinaci)
Spinacia oleracea

Spinach is a hearty green much appreciated in Italy. It is also very nutritious, as it is chock full of vitamins (especially vitamins A and B2) and minerals such as iron and calcium.

HOW TO GROW: If the weather is cool and the soil is rich and filled with humus, spinach is easy to grow. Since spinach is a cool-season crop, many varieties quickly go to seed if the weather is too warm. Sow seeds in early spring or fall, or in winter in mild-winter areas. Plant seeds ½ inch (13 mm) deep about 1 inch (2.5 cm) apart, in full sun in rich, well-drained soil. Keep them fairly moist. Thin seedlings to 3 inches (8 cm) apart and use the thinnings in salads. Make successive sowings every two or three weeks to extend the harvest. Spinach has occasional problems with slugs and leaf miners, plus downy mildew under fall and winter conditions. Harvest leaves a few at a time as needed by cutting or pinching them off, or harvest the entire plant.

Spinach

VARIETIES
Spinach varieties vary in leaf type—smooth or savoyed—heat tolerance, mildew resistance, and strength of taste. As a rule, smooth-leafed spinaches tolerate heat better than savoyed ones, and savoyed leaves are harder to clean. The Italians grow both types.
Bloomsdale: 48 days, old-time variety, savoyed leaves, heavy-yielding, slow to bolt
Italian Summer: 40 days, bolt-resistant, semi-savoyed leaves are easy to clean, good flavor, high-yielding, resistant to downy mildew
Olympia: 45 days, dark green smooth leaf, slow to bolt, mildew-resistant
Tyee: 45 days, hybrid variety, dark green savoyed wrinkled leaves, upright vigorous growth, slow to bolt, tolerant of mildew, good for most seasons

HOW TO PREPARE: First some generalities about spinach. When cooking it, avoid aluminum or iron containers, as spinach picks up a metallic taste. Spinach is very nutritious, but is also high in oxalic acid, which in large amounts ties up calcium and can impair kidney function. Therefore, it is best not to eat it in large amounts. Spinach seems to attract more than its share of sand and soil, so to enjoy it, it's critical to wash spinach well.

Spinach is very popular in Italy. Young tender leaves are used raw in salads, either alone or combined with lettuces and other greens. When cooked spinach is usually boiled in salted water and drained, with the extra water squeezed out. Sometimes Italians combine spinach with chard leaves or many of the so-called "wild greens." They generally serve it reheated in olive oil, garlic, and seasonings or use the cooked spinach, with or without other greens. It is added to a soup with barley and cannellini beans; combined with pancetta, tomatoes, and herbs for a pasta sauce; chopped and used in a soufflé; used in fillings for ravioli; stewed with squid and tomatoes; pureed and incorporated in pastas of many types; enjoyed as a side dish; or incorporated into a gratin.

SQUASH, SUMMER
(zucchini, zucchette)
Cucurbita pepo var. *melopepo*

SQUASH, WINTER AND PUMPKINS
(zucche)
C. maxima, C. moschata, C. pepo

The most famous Italian squash is zucchini; even the name is Italian. There are unique Italian zucchinis of different colors and shapes, and some with flowers that are particularly well suited for sautéing or stuffing.

HOW TO GROW: All the squashes are warm-season annuals. In short-summer areas seeds must be started indoors. The plants are usually grown in hills measuring about 3 feet (0.9 m) across, with two or three plants to a hill. Space hills 5–6 feet (1.5–1.8 m) apart for summer squash, and 7–10 feet (2.1–3 m) apart for winter squash and pumpkins. Squash needs rich humus, full sun, and ample water during the growing season. It also benefits from regular applications of fish emulsion or a balanced organic fertilizer that is not too high in nitrogen. Do not let the plants dry out, and keep young plants well weeded.

Squash may be afflicted with squash bugs or spotted and striped cucumber beetles. Squash vine borers can also be a problem east of the Rockies. Mildew is the most common disease of this group and is to be expected by the end of the season.

Pick summer squash when it is quite young and tender; in its "adolescent" stage when the blossoms have just withered, indicating that the squash is still

'Tromboncino'

Liming may be needed every few years if you live in an area with acidic soil. Tomatoes prefer a soil pH between 6 and 7. Keep your tomato plants evenly watered. Deep, fairly infrequent waterings are best. Mulch with compost after the soil has warmed up thoroughly.

A few major pests afflict tomatoes, including tomato hornworms, cutworms, tobacco budworms, nematodes, and whiteflies. A number of diseases are fairly common to tomatoes, including fusarium and verticillium wilt, alternaria, and tobacco mosaic. Control diseases by rotating crops, planting resistant varieties, and practicing good garden hygiene.

Harvest tomatoes as they ripen. Color and a slight give to the fruit are the best guides to ripeness. Remove fruit from the plant with care not to break stems bearing fruit. Harvest with a slight twist of the wrist or with scissors or shears.

VARIETIES

In a catalog, the capital-letter abbreviation after the name of the variety indicates the disease resistance. For example, VF or VFF indicates resistance to some strains of verticillium and fusarium wilt. Other initials include N for nematodes; T or TMV for tobacco mosaic virus; and A for alternaria.

Tomato varieties are either "determinate" or "indeterminate." Determinate plants are those in which the vines grow little or not at all once the fruit is set. They usually need little support, and you can expect the fruit to ripen within a short time. Indeterminate vines continue to grow after the first fruit is set, and they continue to set new fruit throughout the season. They need staking or other support, and their fruit ripens over a long period of time.

Medium to Large Red Tomatoes

Bissignano #2: 78 days, large juicy Italian slicing tomato, good flavor, plum or globe shape; can also be used for cooking; larger, indeterminate, high-yielding plants

Costolulto Genovese: 80 days, Italian heirloom, delicious slightly tart flavor, large—1 pound (0.45 kg) and up—deep red, lobed fruits from the Piedmont region of Italy, for slicing or cooking, vigorous productive indeterminate vines, resistant to verticillium and fusarium wilt

Gigante Liscio: large red smooth-globed fruits with the green shoulders appreciated in Italy, determinate vigorous plants, good disease resistance

Marmande VF: 67 days, semi-determinate, tolerates cool weather, delicious meaty beefsteak-type fruit

Processing Tomatoes

La Rossa VFF: 75–78 days, great-tasting Italian-type sauce and paste tomato, very thick walls, little juice, cooks down very quickly, determinate

Milano: 63 days, early Italian hybrid, plum-type with rich tomato taste for sauce, drying, and can-

'San Marzano' Tomatoes

LEFT TO RIGHT: 'Costoluto Genovese' tomatoes, yellow and red paste tomatoes, and Roma tomatoes

ning; compact determinate bushes, high yields, resistant to verticillium and fusarium wilts

Principe Borghese: 75 days, small heirloom determinate plants with numerous small fruits, grown in Italy for drying—in some areas houses are decorated with long bunches drying in the sun, not very disease-resistant

Roma VF: 78 days, determinate, improved cultivar of old 'Roma' with considerably more disease resistance, large harvests of thick-walled fruits ideal for sauces, paste, and canning

San Marzano: 75 days, heirloom, indeterminate, oblong great-tasting paste tomato, good for canning or drying, vigorous plants, considered the "gold standard" for flavor in Italy, the F1 hybrid 'Super Marzano VFNT' is more pear shaped, determinate, and very productive

San Remo: 76 days, Italian hybrid, very large sauce or drying tomatoes, tall indeterminate vines, high yields, resistant to verticillium and fusarium

Viva Italia VFFNA: 80 days, pear-shaped fruit with high sugar content, for fresh eating, canning, or freezing; determinate plants are highly disease- and heat-resistant

HOW TO PREPARE: In Italy large slicing tomatoes are generally eaten raw, sometimes served with olive oil and fresh basil. The paste (or plum) tomatoes are preferred for cooking. Favorite herbs to use with tomatoes are basil, oregano, marjoram, and parsley. Tomatoes can be stuffed with all sorts of fillings, from risotto to pasta to tuna and black olives, as is popular in southern Italy. Cooked dishes that feature tomatoes include *peperonata* (tomatoes, peppers, and onions braised in butter and served with meat or a frittata); a soup with garlic, mushrooms, and basil that's ladled over bread; bread salad with onions and basil; and a tomato pizza with mozzarella cheese. Tomatoes are also integral to many pasta dishes. A common pasta sauce is one in which a vegetable such as spinach, artichoke pieces, zucchini, or eggplant chunks are combined with pancetta or prosciutto and seasonings and served over compact types of pasta and served with Parmesan cheese. In parts of the south a little hot pepper may be added to the sauce. In the summer the sauce is made with fresh tomatoes, in the winter from canned tomatoes or tomatoes that were pureed and dried in the sun.

In Italy dried tomatoes are not usually found in cooked dishes, as they might be in the United States. Instead, they are marinated in olive oil, sometimes with added seasonings, and used as a snack or condiment or in an antipasto.

Cooking from the Garden

Italian cuisine is glorious! The bounty of Italy's vegetable varieties defies description, and delicious ways of preparing them seem almost endless. It is not difficult to enjoy a diet that is both Italian and meatless. With so many tasty options for enjoying vegetables with pasta, rice and pizza dishes—not to mention on their own—both vegetarian and vegan diets are at home in Italian cuisine.

Considered the "mother cuisine" for much of Europe, it has its roots in ancient Rome. Cabbages, artichokes, broccoli, peas, chard, lettuce, fennel, mint, parsley, melons, and apples, as well as wine and cheese, many kinds of meat, and grains were all enjoyed by ancient Romans. For feasts Roman cooks used many spices, developed recipes for cheesecake and omelets, and roasted all types of meat. From this noble beginning a sophisticated and flavorful cuisine has emerged.

After the excesses of the Roman banquets, at which quantity was more important than quality, centuries of cooks on the Italian peninsula selected the best of the ancient cuisine and continued to pursue the art of cooking. In the late Middle Ages Italian cooks perfected bread making and started making pasta. In the sixteenth century the first modern cooking school was opened in Florence, and from then on cooking has remained a high art in Italy and cooks have continued to explore new ingredients and new ways to prepare foods. In fact, Italian chefs were the first to embrace many of the foods of the New World in the early 1500s. Italians quickly learned to appreciate snap beans, tomatoes, peppers, squash, and potatoes; eventually these wonderful vegetables found their way into much of European cooking.

Eggplant and the herb nepitella are classic Italian ingredients. Here (**LEFT**) the eggplant has been grilled and finished with a little nepitella butter.

LEFT: A pantry for Italian cooking would be remiss if it didn't include extra-virgin olive oil, Parmigiano-Reggiano cheese, garlic, rosemary, tomatoes, and pasta.
BELOW: Melons, tomatoes, onions, and beans from my garden

While most Italians share a somewhat similar basis for their cuisine, the foods in one part of Italy are often quite different from those in another, because of regional differences in history, economics, and climate. (Remember, Italy was but a group of nation-states a little more than a hundred years ago.) For example, in northern Italy cooks use quite a bit of butter and cream. Pasta there often contains eggs and is rolled out into flat noodles. A specialty of Piedmont, near the French border, is *bagna cauda*, a rich sauce made with cream, butter, garlic, and anchovies. Traditionally, the Piedmontese dip strips of cardoon in *bagna cauda*, but they also use fennel, cauliflower, and peppers. Near Venice, in Treviso and Verona, the bitter chicories (radicchios) are much prized; they are enjoyed as salad greens or sometimes roasted. In nearby Padua fritters are made with squash blossoms. Vegetables abound in Rome and vicinity, where broccoli is cooked in wine, olive oil, and garlic; little peas are served in spring, sometimes cooked with tiny morsels of prosciutto and served on pasta; and white beans are baked with pork rinds. Most of these dishes would not be found in more southern parts of Italy.

The dishes of southern Italy are, as a rule, more heavily spiced than those of the north, redolent of basil, oregano, garlic, and sometimes hot peppers. The primary cooking oil is made from olives, because butter is not as easily obtained, as cows do not produce well in the hot, dry climate. Sauces are often made with sun-ripened tomatoes and olive oil. The primary pastas are dried and tubular and usually do not contain eggs. A favorite dish of Naples, considered the center of southern Italian cooking, is a sauce for pasta made with tomatoes, onions, garlic, and often some type of meat. A fish soup from Abruzzi contains onions, tomatoes, garlic, bay leaves, and parsley. Throughout much of southern Italy, the favorite vegetables are red peppers, eggplant, tomatoes, spinach, and artichokes.

Over the years, as Italian cuisine has been refined, it has not evolved into one filled with complex dishes, as is common in much of France. Instead, it has remained elegantly simple. Italian cuisine is often described as unadorned and honest; as Waverley Root, food writer, comments, "The apparently simple cooking of Italians is, in fact, more difficult at times to achieve than the more elaborate refined French cooking. Things have to be good in themselves, without aid, to be exposed naked." In his book *The Cooking of Italy*, he adds, "Fruits and vegetables must be picked at the right time, neither one day too early nor too late. They must not travel far, must not be preserved beyond their allotted season by chemicals and refrigeration."

Given Waverley Root's comments, you can see why a garden of fresh, well-grown vegetables and herbs becomes a critical part of truly fine Italian cooking. In addition, since Italian cuisine is so unadorned, not only the vegetables and herbs, but also all the starting ingredients must be the best. When you prepare the recipes that follow, use only the highest-quality olive oil—cold-pressed, extra virgin for both salads and cooking. The Parmesan

and other cheeses must also be of the best quality; canned or generic versions obliterate rather than highlight the flavor of your vegetables. Visit a good Italian delicatessen to stock up on superior olives and olive oils, arborio rice, polenta, fontina, and Parmigiano-Reggiano cheeses, and anchovies preserved in salt. These items may seem expensive at first, but you will use only small amounts of these ingredients, and they make a startlingly big difference in your cooking. If you don't have access to such specialties, there are a number of online suppliers (see Resources, page 109).

Seasonal Dining

Of all the modern cuisines, I find Italian the most married to the garden. The Italian diet is still blessedly seasonal. This truth came home to me the first time I visited Italy, when nearly every restaurant we went to for three weeks in April offered artichokes, spring greens, and peas. There were no roasted bell peppers or pears or snap beans on the menu—the vegetables offered were spring vegetables, period. Further, Italian cooking relies upon a variable harvest. A hurried garden harvest can always produce a fabulous meal. The meals are suited to what a garden produces—a small handful of spinach, a few small heads of broccoli, and the season's last two carrots would work in a salad, or they could be sautéed and served with polenta or pasta and sprinkled with cheese. Most recipes don't call for a pound of this and a pound of that; often the ingredients list is fluid.

One final thought: while much of Italian garden cooking strikes us as rustic, or home cooking, in Italian cuisine more than any other, fresh vegetables and herbs can also be haute cuisine. In Giuliano Bugialli's *Foods of Italy*, for example, you can find recipes for vegetable compote with dry zabaione, pepper salad with capers, and carabaccia "of the full moon," made with fresh peas, carrots, and fennel. Bugialli goes on to say, "Vegetables, even more than pasta, are the cornerstone of Italian cooking." With the produce from your Italian garden, you can now truly create the tastes of Italy.

The ideal time to harvest tomatoes is when they're ripe on the vine

Preparation Methods

Vegetables in Italy are cooked in endless ways, befitting their status. They are included in every part of the meal, from antipasto to an occasional dessert.

Antipasto

Translated into English, *antipasto* means "before the meal," and it's associated more with restaurants than with home cooking. While an antipasto can consist of olives, anchovies, sliced meats, and seafoods, many vegetables are served as well. Some of these are white beans with seasonings, sometimes made into a puree and served on toasted bread; roasted red bell peppers served alone or with capers; pickled cherry peppers; thin slices of fennel drizzled with olive oil; chopped tomatoes and basil on toasted bread; and all sorts of vegetables in a tomato sauce. They can be offered in conjunction with other seafood or meat dishes for a party or served singly in a family setting.

Soups

Soups appear to be the "soul food" of Italy. They are generally a hearty mix of vegetables and seasonings thickened with either pasta, rice, or bread. Minestrone, which translates to "big soup," is this type of soup. There are also soups that feature only one or two vegetables. Meat is rare in an Italian soup; sometimes just a little prosciutto is added for flavor. Many soups are served warm in the winter, and at room temperature in the summer. As a rule, the soups in the north are hearty and fairly filling whereas the ones in the south tend to be lighter.

ABOVE: Like the tomatoes and the zucchini itself, zucchini flowers can be enjoyed raw as well as cooked.
OPPOSITE: Vegetables are an integral part of an Italian antipasto. This one includes slightly cooked romanesco broccoli, roasted pimento peppers, sprouting broccoli, and sliced fennel.

Salads

Salads are very popular in Italy. They are most often a simple presentation of lettuces, endive, escarole, arugula, and all sorts of chicories (either alone or in a mixture) drizzled with premium olive oil and salt. Mixed, young, tangy "wild greens" are popular in the spring and are simply dressed with olive oil and salt. Vinegar or lemon juice is sometimes added, as are fresh herbs and, occasionally, garlic.

Pinzimonio is the name of a dressing made with the best possible quality of olive oil and served in a small bowl. Diners season the oil to their taste with salt and pepper and then dip raw vegetables into it, most commonly wedges of bulbing fennel, but paper-thin slices of raw artichokes, sliced radicchio, bell peppers, and tomatoes are also favored. At home, *pinzimonio* usually features one vegetable, though Italian restaurants often offer a mix.

Another lovely Italian salad is the Tuscan bread salad *panzanella*. Soak slightly stale rustic bread in water for about five minutes, squeeze the bread with your hands to remove the water, and then crumble the bread into the bottom of a large salad bowl. Over this spread fresh ripe tomatoes, sliced onions, and basil. Pour a dressing of olive oil, wine vinegar, and seasonings over the vegetables, toss the salad, and serve it at room temperature. In some areas shrimp or squid is added to the vegetables.

Side Dishes

Most fresh vegetables are generally cooked in the same manner, whether they are used as the basis of a side dish, say, or added to a pasta dish. A large pot of salted water is brought to a boil and vegetables are cooked until just tender. They are then drained. Leafy greens are then squeezed to remove excess water. Vegetables can be refreshed by warming them in a pan with butter or olive oil just before serving, or baking them with a drizzle of oil and a sprinkling of cheese. Often, garlic, anchovies, or herbs are added to the oil, and freshly grated Parmesan cheese is sprinkled on before serving or it is passed at the table.

Sometimes vegetables are used in combination, such as peas and artichokes, potatoes with bulbing fennel, and zucchini with peppers. Another common presentation is cooking a little prosciutto or pancetta and garlic in olive oil and adding cooked snap beans, zucchini, or fava beans.

Both cherry and paste types of tomatoes can be dried

In Italy vegetables are also grilled, braised, and baked. Grilling them over charcoal or gas has become popular in Italy in the past few decades. Some favorites are radicchio wedges, eggplant slices, zucchini, peppers, and tomatoes, grilled with a little olive oil and seasonings. They often accompany grilled meats and fish and sometimes are served with a flavored butter or a dipping sauce. Braising vegetables, often in a tomato sauce, has a long history in Italy. Zucchini and snap beans are favorite candidates for braising, as are endive, cabbage, and greens such as spinach and chard. Asparagus, artichokes, and cauliflower are enjoyed baked with a béchamel sauce or a drizzle of olive oil or butter and topped with grated cheese and/or bread crumbs.

Pasta

Pasta, a seemingly simple combination of wheat flour and water, is a beloved food in much of Italy. It is formed into many shapes—from bow ties, spirals, "ears," rice shapes, and long strings to large, flat lasagna noodles—from either fresh dough or, much more commonly, dried. Today there are dozens of dried pastas available worldwide—most are of very high quality—and numerous types and varieties of fresh pasta are available from specialty food shops.

For many Italians, pasta is a daily staple. For the past few hundred years a pasta course has often started the meal. And the dressings for pasta seem endless. While meats, seafood, mushrooms, and cheeses are common, many vegetables are also featured with pasta—and not just the ubiquitous tomatoes. It's not uncommon for the vegetables in the north of Italy to be prepared with butter, cream, or cheese. In the south vegetables are more often dressed with olive oil and seasonings. Generally the long thin noodles are served with light, slippery sauces that keep the noodles from sticking together; more substantial vegetable accompaniments are usually served with short pastas such as penne, rigatoni, orecchiette, or fusilli. These shorter noodles are also favored for baking.

Pasta is critical to Italian cuisine. Pictured here (**ABOVE, CLOCKWISE FROM THE TOP LEFT**) are farfalle, penne, gemelli, orecchiette, rigatoni, garlic pasta, fusili, conchiglie, and tricolor radiatore.

When you think of pasta and vegetables, it's amazing to examine all the possibilities. There are spinach, arugula, and wild greens with olive oil and seasonings, tossed with penne pasta; rigatoni pasta with broccoli, olive oil, and garlic; asparagus, fava beans, and broccoli raab with orecchiette; fusilli with arugula and tomatoes; peas and ham with a cream sauce on fettuccine; and baby artichokes with pancetta. Then there is pasta with leeks and lemons, or radicchio and shrimp, squash blossoms and garlic, and Tuscan black kale and potatoes—they all grace Italian tables in different regions.

When preparing pasta, a useful rule of thumb is 2 ounces (57 g) of dried or 4 ounces (113 g) of fresh pasta per person for a traditional Italian pasta course, and nearly double that amount for a main dish. Cook the pasta in a very large pan, using 6 quarts (5.7 l) of salted water for every pound (454 g) of pasta. (If you are parboiling vegetables, in Italy it is common to first use the water to cook the vegetables and then the pasta.) Add the pasta to the already boiling water and

cook until the pasta is *al dente*, or just barely tender, which may be from as little as 30 seconds for a fresh small pasta to 13 minutes or longer for large dry pastas. Stir the pasta occasionally. Drain the pasta only fleetingly so a small amount of cooking water still coats the noodles. Transfer the pasta to a warm bowl and immediately dress it with olive oil and seasoning, butter, cheese, or the sauce, tossing to prevent the noodles from sticking together. In Italy the usual proportion is 2 tablespoons (30 ml) of sauce to one portion of pasta. Americans usually like more sauce.

Although we usually think of pasta as a hot dish, there are many recipes for pasta salads. The pasta is dressed before it cools, and seasonings and vegetables are added. The dish is then refrigerated. One of my favorite lunches is leftover pasta. The following day I sauté it with a little olive oil to which I add chopped garlic, onions, and a few chopped herbs such as chives, parsley, rosemary, basil, and oregano. When lightly brown I sprinkle the pasta with a little freshly grated romano cheese. Yum.

Interview:

Paul Bertolli

When I met Paul Bertolli, he was the chef at Chez Panisse Restaurant in Berkeley, California. He later became chef and owner of Oliveto Restaurant in Oakland. In 2006 he founded Fra' Mani, which specializes in the manufacture of old-world Italian foods (www.framani.com)

I went to Paul years ago for in-depth information on Italian cooking because I knew that Italian

food had become his great interest. For five years Paul had cooked and traveled in Italy. During his stay in Italy, Paul worked with vegetables from the Florence produce market while cooking at restaurants in that city, and he also cooked with vegetables from an extensive garden at Villa la Pietra, a private residence where he was chef. I asked Paul to share his thoughts on Italian vegetables and their preparation and then talk about some of the individual vegetables.

The vegetable garden at Villa la Pietra was staffed by four gardeners. While there, Paul saw a few vegetables he'd never seen before, such as Tuscan black cabbage (a green to black or forest green member of the cabbage family that sends up large, slightly curled leaves from a thick central stem), artichokes with purple buds, and a number of greens and herbs that were gathered from the wild. But he was most impressed that the vegetables—even those that might be considered common—"were just really so good; great little string beans, red and white shelled beans, and the tomatoes all were outstanding."

In Italy, "a common way to feature certain fresh vegetables, such as mushrooms, fennel, celery, and radishes, is to slice them very thinly," Paul explained. Italians do this, for instance, when making a salad. Back in the United States Paul uses a refined method in which he shaves the vegetables with a mandoline. To protect your hand when using a mandoline, be sure to wear an oven mitt or use a mandoline guard.

One vegetable often sliced in Italy is the artichoke. "In Italy," Paul said, "I saw artichokes with purple buds. They were wonderful eaten raw." To prepare an artichoke for slicing, remove the tough outside leaves, cut off the top and most of the stem, pare the leaves remaining at the base, and slice it very thinly or shave it on a mandoline. Cut from the stem to the top of the artichoke. You'll end up with a pile of shavings that look similar to planed wood. Because artichokes discolor very soon after they are cut, be prepared to serve them immediately. Just before serving them, drizzle on virgin olive oil, season with salt and pepper, and add a few drops of lemon juice; then make thin shavings of Parmesan cheese with a cheese slicer and scatter the cheese on top. For a variation, top slices of *bresaola*, very thinly sliced air-cured beef, with dressed artichokes cut in a similar manner.

One of Paul's favorite vegetables is fennel. When it's more fibrous, he likes to string it like celery. "Or, instead, you can just use the inner heart," he said. "In this country, I feel fennel isn't used enough. It has such a sweet flavor and goes well with so many other vegetables. It too can be served shaved, like the artichoke salad."

Paul said he tried several different varieties of chicory when he lived in Treviso, near Venice. "I think the best I ever had were 'Verona' chicories that were very bitter because they had been left growing at the sides of the fields since the previous season and had not been blanched. Many Italians in the countryside eat the bitter chicories, but what you generally see commercially in the markets are the milder, blanched types of all those chicories. I don't care for the market varieties; I prefer a strong, bitter flavor. As a chef, you're always dealing with things that have these fine flavors. When I eat a strong chicory, I prefer to slice it very thinly. The dressing coats the sliced chicory more thoroughly, and this makes it seem less bitter. Sliced chicory is good combined with thinly sliced onions and drizzled with good red wine vinegar." Paul also likes the Catalonian-type chicory, which Italians tie up and grill. After grilling it, they usually serve it topped with anchovies, onions, and olive oil.

Cime di rapa, or broccoli raab, Paul noted, is sometimes picked in Italy when it is tiny and leafy. Italians steam *cime di rapa* and use it as a nest for loin of pork, which is usually spit-roasted or braised.

In Italy arugula is used primarily in salads, but Paul sometimes likes to use it as a seasoning or herb. For instance, he uses it in ravioli: "I make pigeon ravioli and add a little arugula. I also use it on celeriac soup. It's a wonderful garnish."

Finely slicing or shaving fresh vegetables releases their natural flavor. Here, a delicious artichoke salad is embellished with olive oil and lemon.

Gifts from the Italian Garden

This section includes recipes for Italian vegetables and herbs. Most are authentically Italian, but I must confess that, like most good cooks and gardeners, I can't resist taking the principals and sometimes giving them my own stamp.

Basil in Parmesan

This recipe, from Rose Marie Nichols McGee, of Nichols Garden Nursery in Oregon, is a great way to preserve the taste of basil for the winter. It's been so popular, she's had it in her herb catalog since 1982. As she says, "I never tire of fresh tomatoes sprinkled with this blend. Use it on salads, pasta, and fresh or cooked tomato dishes. This recipe makes a good basis for a later preparation of pesto. Small jars frozen and presented as gifts later in the year will be much appreciated." It stays fresh in the refrigerator for one week. Freeze it for longer storage.

Makes about 2 cups (app 225g)

1 bunch fresh green basil
Approximately ¾ cup (75 g) Parmesan cheese, freshly grated

Rinse the basil and dry it in a salad spinner. Roll a handful of basil leaves into a bunch and with a sharp knife cut the leaves into a thin chiffonade. Repeat the process with the rest of the basil. You should have about 1½ cups (150 g) chopped. In a half-pint canning jar with a tight-fitting lid, layer ¼ inch (7 mm) of Parmesan cheese on the bottom, then layer ¼ inch (7 mm) of basil, then layer another ¼ inch (7 mm) of Parmesan, and so on. Press down firmly on the top to remove any air pockets, and then sprinkle on a final layer of Parmesan.

Nepitella Butter

Try this butter melted over steamed artichokes and carrots and in all sorts of fish or poultry dishes. In Italy nepitella is often paired with eggplant and mushrooms. The butter may be frozen for up to three months.

Makes ½ cup

1 small handful of nepitella
4 ounces (113 g) sweet butter (1 stick), room temperature
1 teaspoon finely grated lemon zest

Wash the nepitella leaves well—examine them for critters. Gently pat dry the leaves in a towel. With a very sharp knife mince the leaves. (Mincing is easier if you gather the leaves into a small ball before cutting them.) You need about 2 tablespoons of finely chopped leaves.

Cut the stick of butter into 6 or 8 pieces and then with a fork slowly work the butter into the nepitella and lemon zest, mashing to incorporate them. Use a rubber spatula to put the mixture into a small butter crock or decorative bowl. Refrigerate until serving time.

CAUTION: There is some evidence that large amounts of nepitella-related plants can cause miscarriage, so pregnant women should avoid it.

Roasted Pimientos

Dried Tomatoes

Mozzarella Marinated with Garlic,
Dried Tomatoes and Basil (see page 74)

Pickled Capers

Pickling is one of a number of ways to preserve capers. Pickled capers can be used on pizza, in sauces, on sliced tomatoes, and with smoked salmon. Let the caper buds sit in a dark place for a few hours before pickling.

1 quart fresh caper buds
1½ cups (375 ml) white wine vinegar
1 teaspoon mustard seeds
1 teaspoon dill seeds
⅓ cup (67 g) packed brown sugar
1 teaspoon salt
1 teaspoon celery seeds
1 garlic clove, crushed

Wash the capers and distribute them among sterilized canning jars. In a saucepan (avoid aluminum, which discolors the buds), combine the remaining ingredients with ½ cup (120 ml) water, bring to a rolling boil, and boil rapidly for 10 minutes. Strain the vinegar mixture and bring it to a boil again. Remove from the heat immediately. Pour the boiling mixture over the capers. Seal the jars tightly and store them for at least two weeks before using.

Dried Tomatoes

Dried tomatoes have an intense flavor and can be used in a multitude of recipes, from vinaigrettes to sauces and soups. They keep for months in a cool, dark, dry place or when frozen. If you have a problem with meal moths, store the tomatoes in the freezer. To soften and rehydrate them for use in sandwiches and sauces, pour boiling water or stock over them and let them sit for a few minutes, or until the skins are soft. The liquid from the rehydrated tomatoes is great for adding flavor to dishes.

Wash the tomatoes and drain them dry. Cut the tomatoes in half (cut 2–3 inch/5–8 cm paste tomatoes into three or four slices) and place them skin-side down on the dehydrator tray. Put the tray in the food dehydrator and follow the directions for drying tomatoes. Different models have different heat- and time-setting recommendations.

If you have a gas oven with a pilot light, you can put the tomatoes on racks and dry them using only the heat from the pilot light (keep the door closed). It takes about 3 days to dry tomatoes this way.

Tomatoes can also be dried in the sun in hot, arid climates. Lay the tomatoes out on a clean window screen that is plastic-coated (or otherwise not made of metal). Place the screen in a very sunny location and cover it with another screen to keep off the flies. Bring the tomatoes in at night to get them out of the dew. Depending on the weather, they will dry in 3–7 days. Dry them until they are leathery and not sticky.

Transfer thoroughly dried tomatoes into zippered, freezer-strength plastic bags. Store them in a cool, dry, dark closet.

Roasted Pimientos

Use these peppers to add zing to your sandwiches, soups, pasta dishes, and sauces.

Makes 1 quart (app 700 g)

Approximately 12 large pimiento peppers
8 garlic cloves
¾–1 cup (180–240 ml) extra-virgin olive oil

Roast the peppers under the broiler or on the grill, peel them, and remove the seeds and stem ends. Layer the peppers in a quart jar with a good seal.

Lightly crush the garlic cloves with the back of a chef's knife. In a small frying pan, heat the oil and slowly sauté the garlic over low heat for about 5 minutes. Do not brown the garlic. Remove the garlic and slowly pour the oil over the peppers. Occasionally run a rubber spatula carefully around the sides of the jar to allow the oil to fill all the air pockets. Refrigerate.

Half an hour before using, take the peppers out of the oil and drain them. Let them come to room temperature and serve them as part of an antipasto or use them in other recipes.

Mozzarella Marinated with Garlic, Dried Tomatoes and Basil

Arrive at the party with this lovely treat or serve it as an appetizer with focaccia or as part of an antipasto. Once the cheese and tomatoes have marinated, use the richly flavored olive oil for dressings or serve it with rustic bread for dipping. These mozzarella balls will keep in the refrigerator for about a week.

Makes 1 quart (app 700 g)

1 cup (55 g) dried tomatoes (see page 73)
¾ pound (341 g) fresh 1-inch (2.5 cm) mozzarella balls
8 garlic cloves, minced, divided
1 teaspoon chopped fresh thyme, divided
1 teaspoon chopped fresh marjoram, divided
1 teaspoon whole green peppercorns or capers, divided
½ teaspoon salt, divided
¼ teaspoon freshly ground black pepper, divided
Approximately 1¼ cups (300 ml) extra-virgin olive oil

In a small bowl, pour 1 cup (240 ml) of boiling water over the dried tomatoes and let them sit for at least 15 minutes, or until they're soft. Drain them and set them aside.

Remove the mozzarella balls from the brine and drain them.

In a quart jar with a lid, layer half the tomatoes on the bottom, then make a layer using half the garlic, herbs, and seasonings. Layer all the mozzarella balls next. Make a top layer of the remaining tomatoes, then the remaining garlic, herbs, and seasonings. Pour the olive oil over the final layer, making sure to cover all the ingredients. Refrigerate to marinate for at least 24 hours.

Misticanza

Generally, *misticanza* is to Italy what *mesclun* is to France—namely, a mix of mostly young salad greens served with a vinaigrette. Historically, *misticanza* is more piquant and bitter than most *mesclun*. *Misticanza* evolved from the practice of gathering wild greens and mixing them in a salad. Today it is a term for a salad of young leaf lettuces, greens, and herbs, either wild or cultivated.

When you have a garden, what goes into your salads depends on what you choose to grow and what is ready to harvest in your garden at any given time.

Serves 6

For the salad:
6 large handfuls of mixed greens
  such as spinach, arugula, corn
  salad, chicories, sorrel, lettuces,
  and frisées
A few leaves of Italian parsley,
  fennel, chervil, mint, or basil

For the vinaigrette:
2–2½ tablespoons (30–45 ml) red
  wine vinegar
1 garlic clove, minced
Salt and freshly ground black
  pepper
5–6 tablespoons (75–90 ml) extra-
  virgin olive oil

To make the salad: Wash the greens and herbs and dry them in a salad spinner. Refrigerate until serving time.

To make the vinaigrette: In a small bowl, mix the vinegar, garlic, salt, and pepper and blend in the oil to taste. Just before serving, toss the dressing gently with the salad and serve.

Classic Minestrone Soup

This minestrone is in the Ligurian style, finished with a flavor burst of rosemary pesto.

Serves 6

3 tablespoons (45 ml) extra-virgin olive oil
1 large yellow onion, sliced
2 (⅓-inch-thick) slices prosciutto, (about ⅓
    –½ pound/151–227 g), julienned
2 large carrots, sliced
8 chard leaves or black kale, washed and
    cut into thin strips
1 small green cabbage, sliced thin
14–16 ripe Italian paste tomatoes, peeled,
    seeded, and chopped, or 3 tablespoons
    (45 ml) sun-dried tomato paste
8 cups (1.92 l) chicken or vegetable stock
3 large garlic cloves, minced
Handful of fresh Italian parsley leaves
Leaves from 2 (3-inch/ app 8 cm) sprigs of
    fresh rosemary
6 tablespoons (45 g) freshly grated
    Parmesan cheese plus extra for garnish
½ dried hot pepper
2 cups cooked cannellini beans, or
    1 (15¼-ounce/ app 435 g) can kidney
    beans
2 handfuls of romano beans, cut into
    1-inch (2.5 cm) pieces
1 small green zucchini, sliced
4 ounces (app 113 g) wide pasta noodles,
    broken into 3-inch (8 cm) pieces
Salt and freshly ground black pepper

In a large stockpot, heat the oil and sauté the onion and prosciutto over low heat until the onions are translucent, about 7 minutes. Add the carrots, chard, cabbage, and tomatoes. Cook together for a few minutes, then add the stock. Cover the stockpot and simmer for about 1¼ hours. The soup can be cooled and then refrigerated (or frozen) at this point.

In the meantime, in a mortar pound the garlic, parsley, rosemary, Parmesan cheese, and hot pepper to a crumbly paste and set it aside.

Half an hour or so before serving, bring the soup to a simmer; add the cannellini and romano beans, zucchini, and pasta; and cook for 5–10 minutes, or until the beans and pasta are tender. Stir in the rosemary mixture, season with salt and pepper, and serve in individual bowls topped with Parmesan cheese, or let diners sprinkle the rosemary pesto over their own bowl.

Bruschetta with Tomatoes and Basil

This rustic appetizer has crunch, complexity, and few calories, and it showcases a classic pairing: basil and tomatoes.

Serves 4

For the bruschetta:
8 thick slices crusty Italian bread
4 garlic cloves (2 peeled, 2 pressed),
  divided

For the topping:
3 tablespoons (45 ml) fruity extra-
  virgin olive oil, divided
16–20 medium fully ripe plum
  tomatoes
2–3 tablespoons finely chopped,
  fresh 'Sweet' or 'Spicy Globe' basil
Salt and freshly ground black pepper
Garnish: sprigs of fresh basil

To make the bruschetta: Toast the bread to a medium brown. While it's still warm, lightly rub one side of each piece with the peeled garlic, using about a quarter clove per piece. Drizzle 2 tablespoons (30 ml) of the olive oil over the toasted bread, dividing it equally among the slices. Set the toast aside, garlic-side up, on a medium-size platter until ready to serve.

To make the topping: Fill a medium-size saucepan half full of water and bring it to a boil. Immerse the tomatoes for 30 seconds, drain and rinse them with cold water, and then peel them. Remove the seeds and chop the tomatoes into half-inch dice. In a small bowl, combine the tomatoes with the pressed garlic, the remaining tablespoon of olive oil, the basil, salt, and pepper. Adjust the seasonings. Set the bowl aside and let the flavors meld for 30 minutes. Before serving, drain the tomato mixture in a sieve for a few minutes.

To serve, spoon a few generous tablespoons of tomatoes on each piece of toast on the garlic-flavored side. Garnish the plate with the fresh basil leaves. Serve immediately.

Radicchio and Corn Salad with Figs and Hazelnuts

This salad is rich and filling, with a nice balance of bitter and sweet. For a party presentation, line the bowl with the radicchio, layer the corn salad on top, and sprinkle on nuts and figs. Dress the salad at the table and toss.

Serves 4 to 6

For the salad:
1 small head radicchio
3 cups (app 600 g) corn salad (mâche)
5 dried figs, divided
¼ cup (2 ounces/ 57 g) hazelnuts
1 tablespoon baking soda

For the dressing:
¼ cup (60 ml) hazelnut or extra-virgin
   olive oil
3 tablespoons (45 ml) balsamic vinegar
Salt and freshly ground black pepper

To make the salad: Tear the radicchio into bite-size pieces. In a large salad bowl, mix it with the corn salad. Coarsely chop two of the figs and add them to the salad; halve the remaining three figs and set them aside.

To peel the hazelnuts, bring 2 cups (480 ml) of water to a boil in a large saucepan. Add the baking soda. Boil the hazelnuts for 5 minutes. Heat the oven to 350ºF/180ºC. Drain and rinse the nuts, and rub off the skins with your fingers. Place the hazelnuts on a cookie sheet and roast them for 10 minutes, or until they're a light brown. Cool the hazelnuts, chop them coarsely, and add them to the salad.

To make the dressing: In a small bowl, whisk together the oil, vinegar, salt, and pepper. Pour the dressing over the salad and toss lightly. Garnish with the fig halves and serve.

Beans, Italian-Style

Preparing beans in the Italian manner means cooking them twice. Bring a large pot of water to a boil, add the beans—be they green or yellow snap beans, romano beans, shelled horticultural beans, or fresh favas—to the water and cook them until they are just tender but still have a hint of crunch. Drain them and then reheat them with flavorings before serving. Butter is sometimes used in this last stage, but a more common finish for the beans is to reheat them in olive oil and garlic and then sprinkle them with Parmigiano-Reggiano cheese. Sometimes mashed anchovies are added to the olive oil.

Serves 4

1 pound (454 g) shelled fresh fava beans (2–2½ pounds (0.9–1.13 kg) of large fava bean pods)
1½ tablespoons (20 ml) of extra-virgin olive oil
2 garlic cloves, minced
Salt and freshly ground black pepper
Freshly grated Parmigiano-Reggiano cheese

In a large saucepan, bring 6–8 cups (1.44–1.92 l) of water to a boil. Add the shelled fava beans and cook them until tender, about 8–12 minutes depending on their size. Pour the beans into a colander and let them cool for a few minutes. If the beans are fairly mature, the outside skin must be removed at this time. Very young beans, ½ inch (13 mm) or so in diameter, need no peeling.

In a small frying pan, heat the oil and sauté the garlic for a few minutes, but do not let it brown. Add the peeled favas and bring them to serving temperature. Lightly salt and pepper the beans. Adjust seasonings, transfer them to a warm bowl, and sprinkle on cheese.

Variations on Italian Beans

Serves 4

1 pound (454 g) green or yellow 'Romano' or snap beans
1½ tablespoons (20 ml) olive oil
2 garlic cloves, minced
Salt and freshly ground black pepper
Freshly grated Parmigiano-Reggiano cheese

Wash and string the beans if necessary. Remove the stem ends. If the beans are large, cut them into 2-inch (5 cm) lengths. Precook the beans as described above. They will cook from 4–7 minutes, depending on their size and age. ('Romano' beans cook more quickly than standard snap beans.) Cook until they are just tender. Drain the beans and proceed as described above.

Classic Broccoli Raab

This variation on a traditional Italian recipe was developed by Joe Queirolo, garden manager of Mudd's Restaurant, in San Ramon, California, and onetime garden manager of my garden. Joe serves the broccoli over orecchiette or polenta.

Serves 4 as a side dish

1 bunch broccoli raab
2 tablespoons (30 ml) extra-virgin
   olive oil
1 or 2 garlic cloves, minced
¼ cup (60 ml) white wine
¼ cup (25 g) grated Pecorino-
   Romano cheese
Salt and freshly ground pepper

Wash the broccoli raab and trim off or peel any coarse stems. Bring a big pot of salted water to a boil. Add the broccoli raab and boil for about 3–5 minutes, or until tender. Drain the broccoli raab and run it under cold water so that it will hold its color.

Meanwhile, heat the oil and sauté the garlic over medium heat until softened, about 1 minute. Add the broccoli raab and toss. Stir in the white wine and let the mixture reduce for 2 or 3 minutes, shaking the pan occasionally. Add salt and pepper to taste. Pour into a serving dish and sprinkle on the cheese; serve immediately.

Grilled Eggplant with Nepitella

Nepitella is a favorite seasoning in some parts of Italy, tasting somewhat like a combination of a mild mint and a little oregano. Use the butter sauce with poultry and with all types of grilled mushrooms as well as with eggplant.

Serves 4 as a side dish

- 1–3 tablespoons (15–45 ml) extra-virgin olive oil
- 1 medium eggplant, cut into ½-inch (13 mm) slices
- 2 tablespoons (28 g) butter
- 1 teaspoon nepitella, minced

With your fingers rub a little olive oil on both sides of each slice of eggplant. You may need more oil, but try not to get the eggplant slices saturated. Grill the eggplant over a medium to hot fire for about 4 minutes on each side, or until slightly brown but not mushy. Meanwhile, melt the butter in a small frying pan and add the nepitella. Transfer the eggplant to a serving dish and drizzle on the nepitella butter.

Tarragon and Balsamic Vinegar–Braised Onions

All sorts of onions are popular in Italy, especially when baked. The addition of balsamic vinegar and tarragon is a bonus. Roasted with just a little olive oil, onions are low in fat and calories and are the perfect appetizer or side dish for a holiday roast.

Serves 6

6 medium red onions, peeled
4 tablespoons (60 ml) extra-virgin olive oil
5 tablespoons (75 ml) balsamic vinegar
1 tablespoon fresh chopped tarragon
Dash of salt
Freshly ground black pepper

Preheat the oven to 350ºF/180ºC. Place the onions in a baking dish, sprinkle them with olive oil, vinegar, tarragon, salt, and pepper. Bake for about 1½–2 hours, or until they're tender and lightly browned. Baste them often with the liquid as they bake.

Grilled Radicchio and Zucchini with Agliata

This a surprisingly delicious way to enjoy vegetables. Radicchio and zucchini have a luscious smoky flavor and sweetness when they're grilled. Serve the vegetables with grilled chicken, steak, or fish. For a vegetarian feast, serve it with polenta and grilled portobello mushrooms.

Serves 4

4 small zucchini
1 large radicchio

For the sauce
1 garlic head and 3 minced cloves, divided
¾ cup (180 ml) and 3 tablespoons (45 ml) extra-virgin olive oil, divided
¾ cup (180 ml) balsamic vinegar
2 cups (app 150 g) day-old Italian rustic bread, crust removed, cubed
2 tablespoons fresh Italian parsley, chopped
¼ teaspoon salt plus extra
Freshly ground black pepper

To make the sauce: Preheat the oven to 350°F/180°C.

With a sharp knife cut off the top of the garlic head until the cloves are exposed. Place the garlic in a small baking dish and sprinkle on 1 tablespoon (15 ml) of the olive oil. Bake the garlic for 20 minutes, or until it's soft. Set it aside.

In a bowl mix the balsamic vinegar and ¼ cup (60 ml) of water. Add the bread cubes and soak them for about 15 minutes or until they're very soft. Squeeze the liquid out of the bread and put the bread into a mixing bowl. Squeeze the roasted garlic from its paper onto the bread. Add one of the minced garlic cloves, and the parsley. Blend all the ingredients into a thick paste. Season with the salt and pepper. Stir in ¾ cup (180 ml) of olive oil, a few drops at a time, to make an emulsion. The oil will not be absorbed completely; a little oil on top is traditional.

To cook the vegetables:
Cut the zucchini lengthwise and quarter the radicchio. Place them in a shallow baking dish. Blend the remaining two minced garlic cloves with the remaining 2 tablespoons (30 ml) of olive oil and brush the zucchini and radicchio with the mixture. Season with salt and pepper. Let the vegetables marinate for at least 1 hour.

Grill the radicchio over a medium flame, turning it often so each side blackens slightly and the vegetables are tender inside, about 10–12 minutes. At the same time grill the zucchini halves on both sides until they're golden and tender, about 10–12 minutes. Transfer them to a warm serving plate. (Instead of grilling them, you may broil the radicchio and zucchini in the oven. Broil at 400°F/200°C for 6–10 minutes, or until golden.)

Serve immediately and pass the agliata sauce for diners to serve themselves.

Risotto-Stuffed Swiss Chard

Large chard leaves are great for stuffing. Serve stuffed chard as a course by itself or as a side dish with meat, fish, and poultry.

Serves 4, three per person.

2 tablespoons (28 g) butter
½ medium onion, chopped
4 ounces (113 g) prosciutto, chopped
1 portobello mushroom, or 6 button mushrooms, chopped
1 cup (225 g) arborio rice
½ cup (120 ml) dry white wine
3–4 cups (720–960 ml) low-salt beef broth
¼ cup (25 g) Parmesan cheese, grated
12 Swiss chard leaves
½ cup (120 ml) tomato sauce
½ cup (54 g) Gruyère cheese

In a heavy saucepan, melt the butter and sauté the onion, prosciutto, and mushrooms over medium heat until tender, about 10 minutes. Add the rice and stir to coat the rice evenly. Add the white wine and simmer, stirring, until the liquid has evaporated. Add the broth, 1 cup (240 ml) at a time, always stirring. Simmer for 20–30 minutes; rice should be al dente. Stir in the Parmesan cheese.

Preheat the oven to 350°F/180°C. Remove the thick lower part of the chard stalks. Steam the leaves for 2 minutes, or until they have wilted. Drain the leaves and rinse them under cold water. Drain them again and place the leaves on paper towels to absorb the moisture. Spoon approximately 2 tablespoons of the arborio mixture onto the middle of each leaf, putting less in smaller leaves. Fold the sides toward the center, then fold in the ends. Make sure the ends overlap to keep the filling secure. Place each package seam-side down in a shallow baking dish that has been brushed with a little olive oil. Spoon tomato sauce over each package. Sprinkle the stuffed chard leaves with the Gruyère and bake them for 20 minutes. Serve immediately.

Fettuccine with Fresh Marinara Sauce

This recipe calls for fettuccine, but any long noodle would work. The sauce is also great on polenta and grilled vegetables. Vary the herbs at whim—try any combination of parsley, tarragon, thyme, fennel, and anise seeds.

Serves 6 to 8 for an Italian pasta course, or 4 to 6 as an American-style entrée.

1 pound (454 g) dry fettuccine noodles
¼ pound (114 g) Parmigiano-Reggiano cheese (not grated)

For the sauce
2 tablespoons (30 ml) extra-virgin olive oil
1 large onion, minced
3 garlic cloves, minced
1 medium Italian bell pepper, roasted, peeled, and chopped
Approximately 20 paste tomatoes, blanched, peeled, seeded, and chopped (app 4 cups/450 g)
1 teaspoon chopped fresh Greek oregano
½ cup chopped fresh basil
Salt and freshly ground black pepper

To make the sauce: In a pan, heat the oil and sauté the onion until transparent, about 7 minutes. Add the garlic and sauté for 3 more minutes.

Add the bell pepper, tomatoes, oregano, and basil, lower the heat, and simmer for about 25 minutes, or until the mixture is fairly thick. Salt and pepper to taste. Makes approximately 3½ cups (840 ml).

To make the noodles: Boil 6 quarts of salted water. Add the fettuccine noodles and stir them for a few seconds to keep them separated. Boil the fettuccine until just barely tender, usually about 11 minutes. Drain the noodles in a colander and immediately pour them into a warm serving bowl. Pour on the warm sauce, toss, and serve immediately. Pass the cheese with a grater so diners can serve themselves.

Penne with Arugula

This is a pasta dish with complexity and a full flavor. It can be served as a pasta course or a light supper.

Serves 4 as a side dish.

2 tablespoons (30 ml) extra-virgin
    olive oil
2 portobello mushrooms, sliced
    (about 2 cups/ 150 g)
3 garlic cloves, minced
6 thin slices (¼–⅓ pound/113–150 g
    total) prosciutto, chopped
4 paste tomatoes, peeled, seeded, and
    chopped (about 2 cups/400 g)
4 cups (app 400 g) young arugula
    leaves
Freshly ground black pepper
4 cups (app 400 g) dried penne
4 tablespoons (25 g) Asiago cheese,
    grated

In a deep frying pan, heat the olive oil and sauté the mushrooms over medium heat for 3–5 minutes, or until the mushrooms are lightly browned. Add the garlic and prosciutto and sauté for 2 more minutes. Reduce heat, add the tomatoes, and simmer for 1 more minute. Add the arugula and toss it in the pan until it has wilted, about 1 minute, then season with pepper.

Meanwhile, bring 3 quarts/liters of salted water to a boil, add the penne, and cook until it's al dente, about 6–9 minutes. Drain the penne. In a warm bowl, toss the penne with the vegetables, and serve with grated Asiago cheese.

Nests with Wild Greens and Fontina

This is a delicious and attractive way to serve an assortment of wild greens. It makes a lovely side dish served with egg dishes or fish, or spooned on crostini to make a beautiful and unusual appetizer. A traditional variation substitutes poached eggs in each nest instead of cheese.

Serves 6

2 pounds (app 907 g) wild mixed greens, such as
    arugula, young borage leaves, dandelion greens,
    spinach, black cabbage, chicory, endive, violet leaves
2 tablespoons (30 ml) extra-virgin olive oil
2 garlic cloves, minced
1 pinch ground red pepper
Salt and freshly ground black pepper
½ cup (50 g) Fontina Val d'Aosta cheese, grated

Preheat the oven to 350°F/180°C. Remove the stems from the greens and wash them thoroughly. Steam them for 3–4 minutes, or until they have wilted. Drain the leaves and rinse them under cold water. Drain them again in a colander, squeezing out the excess water. In a frying pan, heat the olive oil and sauté the garlic over low heat for about 2 minutes. Add the greens, hot red pepper, salt, and black pepper and sauté for 2 more minutes. Let the greens cool to room temperature. Divide them into six equal portions and shape each portion into a ball. Place the balls in a baking dish and with your thumb make an indentation in the center of the ball to form a little nest. Fill the indentation with the grated Fontina cheese. Bake the nests for 5 minutes, or until the cheese has melted.

Savory Bread Pudding with Sorrel and Baby Artichokes

This unusual and complex dish combines the nutty flavors of Swiss cheese and artichokes with the lightness of sorrel, interwoven with layers of fresh herbs. It can serve as the star of the meal served with an endive or beet salad and a good red wine, or accompany filets of salmon or tuna.

Serves 4 as a hearty supper, 6 as a side dish.

1 loaf of rustic Italian bread, or about 12 slices of leftover substantial breads of all types (avoid soft sandwich-type breads, since they tend to produce a gummy dish)

1 tablespoon (15 ml) fresh lemon juice

1 pound (454 g) 2-inch (5 cm) long baby artichokes (approximately 18)

3 cups (920 ml) nonfat or low-fat milk

5 eggs, beaten

1 teaspoon salt

1 teaspoon pepper

¼ cup (25 g) grated Parmesan cheese, divided

4 ounces (113 g) Monterey Jack cheese, slivered, divided

4 ounces (113 g) Emmentaler cheese, slivered, divided

2 tablespoons snipped fresh chives

2 tablespoons chopped fresh Italian parsley

2 tablespoons chopped fresh lemon thyme

1½ cups (app 150 g) chopped sorrel leaves

1 tablespoon (14 g) butter, cut into small pieces

If you're using fresh bread, cut the loaf into 12 equal slices and arrange the slices on two cookie sheets. Bake at 200ºF/93ºC for about 30 minutes, or until dry but not brown. Let the bread cool.

While the bread is in the oven, prepare the artichokes. Partially fill a small bowl with water and add the lemon juice. Peel off any dried or bruised leaves from the artichokes, cut off the top ⅓ inch (8 mm) and discard it, and immediately immerse the artichokes in the lemon water to prevent them from turning brown. Place 1 inch (2.5 cm) of water in the bottom of a steamer and bring it to a boil. Drain the artichokes and put them in the steamer basket, cover, and steam them over medium heat for about 20 minutes, or until they're just tender. Remove them from the heat and set them aside.

Break up the toasted bread slices and put them in a shallow baking dish. Pour the milk over the bread and let it soak for about 20 minutes, stirring the bread around to make sure it absorbs the milk and gets soft. After it has soaked, squeeze the milk out of the bread and set it aside. Pour the leftover milk into a measuring cup, adding more to get to ½ cup (120 ml) if necessary. In a bowl combine the ½ cup (120 ml) cup milk, eggs, salt, and pepper and mix well. Set aside.

Preheat the oven to 350ºF/180ºC. Oil a 3-quart casserole. Layer one third of the bread in the bottom of the casserole. Layer two thirds of the artichokes over the bread, then layer half of the three cheeses combined and then half the sorrel and herbs. Layer another one third of the bread, add the final one third of the artichokes, (reserve a few for the top), the last half of the sorrel and herbs, and the rest of the cheeses, reserving 3 tablespoons (45 ml) for the top. Top the casserole with the last one third of the bread and the reserved artichokes. Pour the milk and egg mixture over the bread, sprinkle on the reserved 3 tablespoons (45 ml) of combined cheeses, and dot with butter.

Bake for about 45 minutes, or until the top is nicely browned and a knife inserted halfway into the middle comes out clean. Serve hot.

Spring Pizza

Pizza can be made with dozens of different vegetables. This particular pizza includes the traditional spring goodies—arugula and artichokes. I prefer a lesser amount of cheese, 6 ounces (170 g), for a lean pizza; other folks prefer their pizza "cheesy" and should use 8 ounces (227 g) of cheese.

Makes 1 medium-size pizza that serves 2

4 baby artichokes
8 dried tomatoes
2 tablespoons (30 ml) extra-virgin olive oil
3 garlic cloves, minced
1 (12-inch/30 cm) prebaked commercial
   pizza shell
6–8 ounces (170–227 g) of fresh mozzarella
   cheese, sliced thin
10 black, dried, *piquées* or kalamata olives,
   pits removed
1 teaspoon fresh oregano, minced
1 cup (app 100 g) young arugula leaves
¾ cup (75 g) Asiago cheese, grated

Preheat the oven to 500°F/260°C. Cut the top ½ inch (13 mm) off the baby artichokes. Cover them with water and simmer them for 10 minutes, or until tender. Cool the artichokes.

While the artichokes are cooking, chop the tomatoes coarsely and reconstitute them in warm water for 10 minutes.

Blend the olive oil with the garlic. Spread the oil mixture evenly over the pizza shell. Distribute mozzarella cheese slices evenly over the pizza shell. Quarter the cooked artichokes and put them on top of the mozzarella. Add the olives and tomatoes and sprinkle them with the oregano. Bake the pizza for 7–10 minutes, or until the cheese has melted. Remove it from the oven, cover it evenly with arugula, and sprinkle on the Asiago cheese.

Either serve the pizza as is or return it to the oven for 2 more minutes to wilt the arugula and melt the Asiago.

Don Silvio's Vegetable Dessert Tart

Vicki Sebastiani, formerly of Viansa Winery, contributed this recipe for a surprisingly rich and delicious dessert made with vegetables.

Serves 6 to 8

For the tart shell:
2 cups (245 g) all-purpose unbleached flour
½ cup (63 g) walnuts, chopped fine
1 cup butter (2 sticks/ 225 g), chilled

For the filling:
2 cups coarsely chopped raw chard leaves
   (about 1 bunch/ 200 g)
2 cups grated zucchini (about 2 medium
   zucchini/ 360 g)
1 cup (150 g) golden raisins
8 leaves chopped fresh mint, or 1 teaspoon
   dried mint
¼ cup (60 ml) honey
4 eggs, lightly beaten
½ cup (120 ml) Viansa Frescolina Chardonnay
   or Savignon Blanc wine

To make the shell: In a bowl, combine the flour and nuts. Add the butter, 2 tablespoons (28 g) at a time, and mix well in food processor until the dough forms a ball. With your fingers spread the dough into a quiche, tart, or pie pan (9–10 inches/22–25 cm in diameter) to ⅛-inch (3 mm) thickness along the bottom and sides and at least ¾ inch (18 mm) up the sides. Chill the shell while you make the filling.

To make the filling: Preheat the oven to 375°F/190°C.

In a large bowl, combine all the filling ingredients. Pour half the filling into a food processor or blender and puree briefly. Combine this portion of the filling with the non-pureed portion of the filling and pour into the shell. Bake the tart for approximately 45 minutes, or until the filling has set (until an inserted knife comes out clean). Cool for 30 minutes before serving. Serve at room temperature.

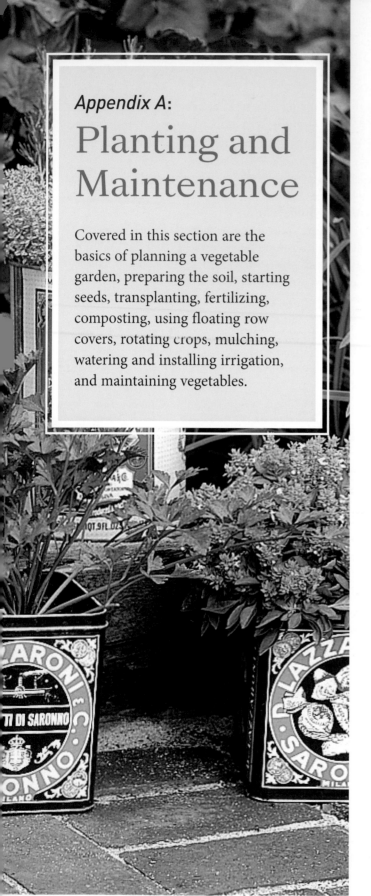

Appendix A:
Planting and Maintenance

Covered in this section are the basics of planning a vegetable garden, preparing the soil, starting seeds, transplanting, fertilizing, composting, using floating row covers, rotating crops, mulching, watering and installing irrigation, and maintaining vegetables.

Planning Your Vegetable Garden

You can interplant a few Italian vegetables and herbs among your ornamentals, or add them to your existing vegetable garden. If you have no vegetable garden, then you need to design one. The first step in planning your vegetable garden is choosing a suitable site. Most chefs recommend locating the edible garden as close to the kitchen as possible, and I heartily agree. Beyond that, the majority of vegetables need at least six hours of sun (eight is better)—except in warm, humid areas, where afternoon or some filtered shade is best—and good drainage. There are only a few Italian edibles that tolerate much shade: Roman mint, arugula, sorrel, and parsley. Annual vegetables need fairly rich soil with lots of added organic matter. They can be planted in rows in a bed by themselves—as part of the classic vegetable garden, say—but some of them, especially eggplants, peppers, radicchios, artichokes, sweet fennel, lettuces, and summer squash, are beautiful and work well interplanted in a flower bed with annual flowers, most of which need the same conditions. In addition, most vegetables can be grown in containers or in large planter boxes.

Once you've decided on where you are going to plant, it's time to choose your vegetables. Your major consideration is, of course, what flavors you enjoy using in the kitchen. With this in mind, look for species and varieties that grow well in your climate. As a rule, gardeners in northern climates and high elevations look for vegetables that tolerate cool and/or short-summer conditions. Many vegetable varieties bred for short seasons and most salad greens are great for these conditions. Gardeners in hot, humid areas require plants that tolerate diseases well, and they need to choose heat-tolerant vegetables.

The USDA Plant Hardiness Zone Map has grouped eleven zones according to winter lows. It is a help in choosing perennial plants, but of only limited use for annual vegetables. The new *Sunset National Garden Book*, published by Sunset Books, gives much more useful climatic information; it divides the continent into forty-five growing zones. Several regional maps describe the temperature ranges and growing season in much detail. The maps are an integral part of this information-packed resource. Of additional interest to the vegetable gardener is the AHS Plant Heat-Zone Map, published by the American Horticultural Society. The heat map details twelve zones that indicate the average number of days each year when

a given area experiences temperatures of 86ºF/30ºC or higher—the temperature at which many plants, including peas and most salad greens, begin to suffer physiological damage. In Italian Garden Encyclopedia (page 25) I indicate which varieties have a low tolerance to high temperatures and those that grow well in hot weather. See Resources (page 109) for information on obtaining the heat map.

In addition to analyzing your climate, knowing what type of soil a particular vegetable needs is equally important. Consider how well your soil drains: is it rich with organic matter and fertility? Poor soil with bad drainage? Is it so sandy that few plants grow well? Find out too what your soil pH is. Nurseries have kits to test your soil's pH, and University Extension Services can lead you to sources of soil tests and soil experts. As a rule, rainy climates have acidic soil that needs the pH raised, and arid climates have fairly neutral or alkaline soil that needs extra organic matter to lower the pH. Most vegetables grow best in soil with a pH of about 6.5—in other words, slightly acidic. Soil that is below 6 ties up phosphorus, potassium, and calcium, making them unavailable to plants; soil with a pH much over 6.5 ties up iron and zinc. Furthermore, is there hardpan under your garden that prevents roots from penetrating the soil, or

water from draining? This is a fairly common problem in areas of heavy clay, especially in many parts of the Southwest with caliche soils—a very alkaline clay. You need answers to these basic questions before you proceed because, to be tender and mild, annual vegetables need to grow fast and with little stress.

Vegetable plants do best with good drainage. Their roots need air, and if the soil stays waterlogged for long, roots suffocate or are prone to root rot. If you are unsure how well a particular area in your garden drains, dig a hole about 10 inches (25 cm) deep and 10 inches (25 cm) across, where you plan to put your garden and fill it with water. The next day fill it again. If it still has water in it eight to ten hours later, you need to find another place in the garden that will drain much faster, amend your soil with much organic matter and mound it up at least 6–8 inches (15–20 cm) above the ground level, or grow your vegetables in containers.

The last consideration is how large a garden you are planning. A few hundred square feet of Italian vegetables like basil, fennel, beans, and eggplant, plus a small bed of Italian lettuces, would give you many classic Italian meals. If you want to get more involved and plant a large garden that might also include Italian tomatoes, broccoli, and zucchini, you need more space

MULCHING

Mulching can save the gardener time, effort, and water. A mulch reduces moisture loss, prevents erosion, controls weeds, minimizes soil compaction, and moderates soil temperature. When the mulch is an organic material, it adds nutrients and organic matter to the soil as it decomposes, making heavy clay more porous and helping sandy soil retain moisture. Mulches are often attractive additions to the garden as well. Applying a few inches of organic matter every spring is necessary in most vegetable gardens to keep them healthy. Mulch with compost from your compost pile, pine needles, composted sawdust, straw, or one of the many agricultural by-products like rice hulls or apple or grape pomace.

COMPOSTING

Compost is the humus-rich result of the decomposition of organic matter, such as leaves and lawn clippings. The objective of maintaining a composting system is to speed up decomposition and centralize the material so you can gather it up and spread it where it will do the most good. Compost's benefits include providing nutrients to plants in a slow-release, balanced fashion; helping break up clay soil; aiding sandy soil to retain moisture; and correcting pH problems. On top of that, compost is free, it can be made at home, and it is an excellent way to recycle our yard and kitchen "wastes." Compost can be used as a soil additive or a mulch.

There need be no great mystique about composting. To create the environment needed by the decay-causing microorganisms that do all the work, just include the following four ingredients, mixed well: three or four parts "brown" material high in carbon, such as dry leaves, dry grass, or even shredded black-and-white newspaper; one part "green" material high in nitrogen, such as fresh grass clippings, fresh garden trimmings, barnyard manure, or kitchen trimmings like pea pods and carrot tops; water in moderate amounts, so that the mixture is moist but not soggy; and air to supply oxygen to the microorganisms. Bury the kitchen trimmings within the pile, so as not to attract flies. Cut up any large pieces of material. Exclude weeds that have gone to seed, because you could promote the growth of those weeds in the garden. Do not add meat, fat, diseased plants, woody branches, or cat or dog manure.

I don't stress myself about the proper proportions of compost materials, as long as I have a fairly good mix of materials from the garden. If the decomposition is too slow, it is usually because the pile has too much brown

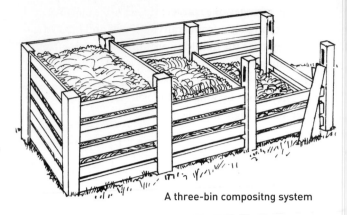

A three-bin compositng system

material, is too dry, or needs air. If the pile smells, there is too much green material or it is too wet. To speed up decomposition, I chop the materials before adding them to the pile and I may turn the pile occasionally to get additional oxygen to all parts. During decomposition, the materials can become quite hot and steamy, which is great; however, it is not mandatory that the compost become extremely hot.

You can make compost in a simple pile, in wire or wood bins, or in rather expensive containers. The size should be about 3 feet (0.9 m) high, wide, and tall for the most efficient decomposition and so the pile is easily workable. It can be up to 5 feet by 5 feet (1.5 m by 15 m), but it then becomes harder to manage. In a rainy climate it's a good idea to have a cover for the compost. I like to use three bins. I collect the compost materials in one bin, have a working bin, and when that bin is full, I turn the contents into the last bin, where it finishes its decomposition. I sift the finished compost into empty garbage cans so it does not leach its nutrients into the soil. The empty bin is then ready to fill up again.

CROP ROTATION

Rotating crops in an edible garden has been practiced for centuries. It's done for two reasons: to help prevent diseases and pests and to prevent depletion of nutrients from the soil, as some crops add nutrients and others take them away.

To rotate crops, you must know what plants are in which families since plants in the same families are often prone to the same diseases and pests and deplete the same nutrients.

The following is a short list of related vegetables.

Goosefoot family *(Chenopodiaceae)*—includes beets, chard, orach, spinach

Cucumber family (gourd) *(Cucurbitaceae)*—includes

cucumbers, gourds, melons, summer squash, winter squash, pumpkins

Lily family (onion) *(Liliaceae)*—includes asparagus, chives, garlic, leeks, onions, Oriental chives, shallots

Mint family *(Lamiaceae)*—includes basil, mints, oregano, rosemary, sage, summer savory, thymes

Mustard family (cabbage) *(Brassicaceae)*—includes arugula, broccoli, cabbages, cauliflower, collards, cresses, kale, kohlrabi, komatsuna, mizuna, mustards, radishes, turnips

Nightshade family *(Solanaceae)*—includes eggplants, peppers, potatoes, tomatillos, tomatoes

Parsley family (carrot) *(Apiaceae)*—includes carrots, celeriac, celery, chervil, coriander (cilantro), dill, fennel, lovage, parsley, parsnips

Pea family (legumes) *(Fabaceae)*—includes beans, cowpeas, fava beans, lima beans, peanuts, peas, runner beans, soybeans, sugar peas

Sunflower family (daisy) *(Asteraceae)*—includes artichokes, calendulas, celtuce, chicories, dandelions, endives, lettuces, marigolds, tarragon

The object is to avoid growing members of the same family in the same spot year after year. For example: cabbage, a member of the mustard family, should not be followed by radishes, a member of the same family, as they are both prone to flea beetles, and the flea beetle's eggs will be in the soil ready to hatch and attack the radishes. Tomatoes should not follow eggplants, as they are both prone to fusarium wilt.

Crop rotation is also practiced to help keep the soil healthy. One family, namely the pea family (legumes), which includes not only peas and beans but also clovers and alfalfa, adds nitrogen to the soil. In contrast, most members of the mustard (cabbage) family deplete the soil of nitrogen. Other heavy feeders are members of the nightshade and cucumber families. Because most vegetables deplete the soil, knowledgeable gardeners not only rotate their beds with vegetables from different families; they also include an occasional cover crop of clover or alfalfa and other soil benefactors like buckwheat and vetch to add what's called green manure. After growing for a few months, these crops are turned under and provide extra organic matter and many nutrients, help stop the pest cycle, and attract beneficial insects. Some cover crops (like rye) are grown over the winter to control soil erosion. The seeds of all sorts of cover crops are available from farm suppliers and specialty seed companies. I've been able to give only the basics on this subject; for more information, see Shepherd Ogden's *Step by Step*

Organic Vegetable Gardening and some of the other basic gardening texts recommended in the "Books and other References" (page 110).

Garden Watering and Irrigation Systems

Even gardeners who live in rainy climates may need to do supplemental watering at specific times during the growing season. Therefore, most gardeners need some sort of supplemental watering system and a knowledge of water management.

There is no easy formula for determining the correct amount or frequency of watering. Proper watering takes experience and observation. In addition to the specific watering needs of individual plants, the amount of watering needed depends on soil type, wind conditions, and air temperature. To water properly, you must learn how to recognize water-stress symptoms (often a dulling of foliage color as well as the better-known symptoms of drooping leaves and wilting), how much to water (too much is as bad as too little), and how to water. Some general rules are:

1. Water deeply. Except for seed beds, most plants need infrequent deep watering rather than frequent light sprinkling.
2. To ensure proper absorption, apply water at a rate slow enough to prevent runoff.
3. Do not use overhead watering systems when the wind is blowing.
4. Try to water early in the morning so that foliage will have time to dry off before nightfall, thus preventing some disease problems. In addition, because of the cooler temperature, less water is lost to evaporation.
5. Test your watering system occasionally to make sure it is covering the area evenly.
6. Use methods and tools that conserve water. When using a hose, a pistol-grip nozzle will shut off the water while you move from one container or planting bed to another. Soaker hoses, made of either canvas or recycled tires, and other ooze and drip irrigation systems apply water slowly and use water more efficiently than do overhead systems.

Drip, or the related ooze/trickle, irrigation systems are advisable wherever feasible, and most gardens are well-suited to them. Drip systems deliver water a drop at a time through spaghetti-like emitter tubes or plastic pipe with emitters that drip water right onto the root zone of each plant. Because of the time and effort

BENEFICIAL INSECTS

In a nutshell, few insects are potential problems; most are either neutral or beneficial to the gardener. Given the chance, the beneficials do much of your insect control for you, provided that you don't use pesticides, as pesticides are apt to kill the beneficial insects as well as the problem insects. Like predatory lions stalking zebra, predatory ladybugs (lady beetles) or lacewing larvae hunt and eat aphids that might be attracted to your lettuce, say. Or a miniwasp parasitoid will lay eggs in the aphids. If you spray those aphids, even with a so-called benign pesticide such as insecticidal soap or pyrethrum, you'll kill off the ladybugs, lacewings, and that baby parasitoid wasp too. Most insecticides are broad spectrum, which means that they kill insects indiscriminately, not just the pests. In my opinion, organic gardeners who regularly use organic broad-spectrum insecticides have missed this point. While it is true they are using an "organic" pesticide, they may actually be eliminating a truly organic means of control, the beneficial insects.

Unfortunately, many gardeners are not aware of the benefits of the predator-prey relationship and are not able to recognize beneficial insects. The following sections will help you identify both helpful and pest organisms. A hand lens is an invaluable and inexpensive tool that will also help you identify the insects in your garden.

Predators and **Parasitoids:** Insects that feed on other insects are divided into two types, the predators and the parasitoids. Predators are mobile. They stalk plants looking for such plant feeders as aphids and mites. Parasitoids, on the other hand, are insects that develop in or on the bodies, pupae, or eggs of other host insects. Most parasitoids are minute wasps or flies whose larvae (young stages) eat other insects from within. Some of the wasps are so small, they can develop within an aphid or an insect egg. Or one parasitoid egg can divide into several identical cells, each developing into identical miniwasp larvae, which then can kill an entire caterpillar. Though nearly invisible to most gardeners, parasitoids are the most specific and effective means of insect control.

The predator-prey relationship can be a fairly stable situation; when the natural system is working properly, pest insects inhabiting the garden along with the predators and parasitoids seldom become a problem. Sometimes, though, the system breaks down. For example, a number of imported pests have taken hold in this country. Unfortunately, when such organisms were brought here, their natural predators did not accompany them. Four pesky examples are Japanese beetles, the European brown snail, the white cabbage butterfly, and flea beetles. None of these organisms has natural enemies in this country that provide sufficient controls. Where they occur, it is sometimes necessary to use physical means or selective pesticides that kill only the problem insect. Weather extremes sometime produce imbalances as well. For example, long stretches of hot, dry weather favor grasshoppers that invade vegetable gardens, because the diseases that keep them in check are more prevalent under moist conditions. There are other situations in which the predator-prey relationship gets out of balance because many gardening practices inadvertently work in favor of the pests. For example, when gardeners spray with broad-spectrum pesticides regularly, not all the insects in the garden are killed—and since predators and parasitoids generally reproduce more slowly than do the pests, regular spraying usually tips the balance in favor of the pests. Further, all too often the average yard has few plants that produce nectar for beneficial insects; instead it is filled with grass and shrubs, so that when a few squash plants and a row of lettuces are put in, the new plants attract the aphids but not the beneficials. Being aware of the effect of these practices will help you create a vegetable garden that is relatively free of many pest problems.

Attracting Beneficial Inserts

Besides reducing your use of pesticides, the key to keeping a healthy balance in your garden is providing a diversity of plants, including plenty of nectar- and pollen-producing plants. Nectar is the primary food of the adult stage and some larval stages of many beneficial insects. Interplanting your vegetables with flowers and numerous herbs helps attract them. Ornamentals, like species zinnias, marigolds, alyssum, and yarrow, provide many flowers over a long season and are shallow enough for insects to reach the nectar. Large, dense flowers like tea roses and dahlias are useless as their nectar is out of reach. A number of the herbs are rich nectar sources, including fennel, dill, anise, chervil, oregano, thyme, and parsley. Allowing a few of your vegetables like arugula, broccoli, carrots, and mustards, in particular, to go to flower is helpful because their tiny flowers full of nectar and pollen are just what many of the beneficial insects need.

Following are a few of the predatory and parasitoid insects that are helpful in the garden. Their preservation and protection should be a major goal of your pest-control strategy.

Ground beetles and their larvae are all predators. Most adult ground beetles are fairly large black beetles that scurry out from under plants or containers when you disturb them. Their favorite foods are soft-bodied larvae like Colorado potato beetle larvae and root maggots (root maggots eat cabbage family plants); some ground beetles even eat snails and slugs. If supplied with an undisturbed place to live, like your compost area or groupings of perennial plantings, ground beetles will be long-lived residents of your garden.

Lacewings are one of the most effective insect predators in the home garden. They are small green or brown gossamer-winged insects that in their adult stage eat flower nectar, pollen, aphid honeydew, and sometimes aphids and mealybugs. In the larval stage they look like little tan alligators. Called aphid lions, the larvae are fierce predators of aphids, mites, and whiteflies—all occasional pests that suck plant sap. If you are having problems with sucking insects in your garden, consider purchasing lacewing eggs or larvae mail-order to jump-start your lacewing population. Remember to plant lots of nectar plants to keep the population going from year to year.

Lady beetles (ladybugs) are the best known of the beneficial garden insects. Actually, there are about four hundred species of lady beetles in North America alone. They come in a variety of colors and markings in addition to the familiar red with black spots, but they are never green. Lady beetles and their fierce-looking alligator-shaped larvae eat copious amounts of aphids and other small insects.

Spiders are close relatives of insects. There are hundreds of species, and they are some of the most effective predators of a great range of pest insects.

Syrphid flies (also called flowerflies or hover flies) look like small bees hovering over flowers, but they have only two wings. Most have yellow and black stripes on their body. Their larvae are small green maggots that inhabit leaves, eating small sucking insects and mites.

Wasps are a large family of insects with transparent wings. Unfortunately, the few large wasps that sting have given wasps a bad name. In fact, all wasps are either insect predators or parasitoids. The miniwasps are usually parasitoids, and the adult female lays her eggs in such insects as aphids, whitefly larvae, and caterpillars—and the developing wasp larvae devour the host. These miniature wasps are also available for purchase from insectaries and are especially effective when released in greenhouses.

PESTS
The following pests are sometimes a problem in the vegetable garden.

Aphids are soft-bodied, small, green, black, pink, or gray insects that produce many generations in one season. They suck plant juices and exude honeydew. Sometimes leaves under the aphids turn black from a secondary mold growing on the nutrient-rich honeydew. Aphids are primarily a problem on cabbages, broccoli, beans, lettuces, peas, tomatoes, and spinach. Aphid populations can build up, especially in the spring before beneficial insects are present in large numbers and when plants are covered by row covers or are growing in cold frames. The presence of aphids sometimes indicates that the plant is under stress—is the cabbage getting enough water, or sunlight, say? Check first to see if stress is a problem and then try to correct it. If there is a large infestation, look for aphid mummies and

Books and Other References

Bianchini, Francesco, Francesco Corbetta, and Marilena Pistoia. *The Complete Book of Fruits and Vegetables.* New York: Crown Publishers, 1975.

Brennan, Ethel, and Georgeanne Brennan. *Sun-Dried Tomatoes.* San Francisco: Chronicle Books, 1995.

Bubel, Nancy. *The New Seed-Starters Handbook.* Emmaus, PA: Rodale Press, 1988.

Bugialli, Giuliano. *Giuliano Bugialli's Foods of Italy.* New York: Stewart, Tabori, and Chang, 1984.

Carr, Anna. *Rodale's Color Handbook of Garden Insects.* Emmaus, PA: Rodale Press, 1979.

Castelvetro, Giacomo. *The Fruit, Herbs, and Vegetables of Italy.* New York: Viking Penguin, 1989.

Cathey, H. Marc. *Heat-Zone Gardening: How to Choose Plants that Thrive in Your Region's Warmest Weather.* Alexandria, VA: Time-Life Custom Publishing, 1998.

Coleman, Eliot. *Four-Season Harvest: How to Harvest Fresh Organic Vegetables from Your Home Garden All Year Long.* White River Junction, VT: Chelsea Green Publishing, 1992.

Creasy, Rosalind. *The Complete Book of Edible Landscaping.* San Francisco: Sierra Club Books, 1982.

Del Conte, Anna. *Gastronomy of Italy.* New York: Prentice Hall, 1987.
——————————. *The Italian Pantry.* New York: Harper and Row, 1990.

De' Medici, Lorenza. T*uscany: The Beautiful Cookbook.* San Francisco: Weldon Owen, 1992.
————————————. *Italy: The Beautiful Cookbook.* Los Angeles: Knapp Press, 1988.

Editors of Sunset Books and Sunset Magazine. *Sunset National Garden Book.* MenloPark, Calif.: Sunset Books, 1997.
————————. *Sunset Western Garden Book.* Menlo Park, CA: Sunset Publishing Corporation, 1995.

Facciola, Stephen. Cornucopia: *A Source Book of Edible Plants.* Vista, CA: Kampong Publications, 1990.

Gilkeson, Linda, Pam Peirce, and Miranda Smith. *Rodale's Pest and Disease Problem Solver: A Chemical-Free Guide to Keeping Your Garden Healthy.* Emmaus, Pa.: Rodale Press, 1996.

Gray, Rose, and Ruth Rogers. *Rogers Gray Italian Country Cookbook.* New York: Random House, 1995.

Harris, Valentina. *Recipes from an Italian Farmhouse.* New York: Simon and Schuster, 1989.

Hazan, Marcella. *Marcella Cucina.* New York: HarperCollins, 1997.

Hill, Madalene, and Gwen Barclay with Jean Hardy. S*outhern Herb Growing.* Fredericksburg, TX: Shearer Publishing, 1987.

La Place, Viana. V*egetables Italian Style: Verdura.* New York: Morrow, 1991.

La Place, Viana, and Evan Kleiman. *Cucina Fresca.* New York: Harper and Row, 1985.

Middione, Carlo. *La Ve ra Cucina: Traditional Recipes from the Homes and Farms of Italy.* New York: Simon and Schuster, 1996.

National Gardening Association. *Gardening: The Complete Guide to Growing America's Favorite Fruits and Vegetables.* Reading, MA: Addison-Wesley, 1986.

Ogden, Shepherd. *Step by Step Organic Vegetable Gardening: The Gardening Classic Revised and Updated.* New York: HarperCollins, 1992.

Olkowski, William, Sheila Daar, and Helga Olkowski. *The Gardener's Guide to Common-Sense Pest Control.* Newtown, CT: Taunton Press, 1995.

Peirce, Pam. *Golden Gate Gardening: A Complete Guide to Year-round Food Gardening in the San Francisco Bay Area and Coastal California.* Seattle: Sasquatch Books, 1998.

Phillips, Roger. *Wild Foods.* Boston: Little, Brown, 1986.

Reilly, Ann. *Park's Success with Seeds.* Greenwood, SC: Geo. W. ParkSeed Co., 1978.

Saville, Carole. *Annuals: A Gardener's Guide."Annual Herbs of the Field Find Home in the Garden."* New York: Brooklyn Botanic Garden Record, 1992.

Scaravelli, Paola, and Jon Cohen. *Cooking from an Italian Garden.* New York: Holt, Rinehart and Winston, 1984.

Teubner, Christian, and Silvio Rizzi and Tan Lee Leng. *The Pasta Bible.* New York: Penguin, 1996.

Willinger, Faith. *Red, White & Greens.* New York: HarperCollins, 1996.

Wolfert, Paula. *World of Food.* New York: Harper and Row, 1988

OTHER REFERENCES

BOOKS
De Laurentis, Giada. *Giada's Italy: My Recipes for La Dolce Vita.* New York: Clarkson and Potter, 2018.

De Laurentis, Giada. *Giada's Kitchen: New Italian Favorites.* New York: Clarkson and Potter, 2008

The Silver Spoon Kitchen. *The Silver Spoon, 2nd ed.* New York: Phaidon Press, 2011.

White, Michael and Andrew Friedman. *Classico e Moderno: Essential Italian Cooking.* New York: Ballantine Books, 2013.

MAGAZINES
Italy Food Magazine https://italyfoodmagazine.com/

Olive Magazine https://www.olivemagazine.com/

MAP
American Horticultural Society Plant Heat Zone Map
http://ahsgardening.org/gardening-resources/gardening-maps/heat-zone-map

Acknowledgments

My garden is the foundation for my books, photography, and recipes. For nearly twelve months of the year we toil to keep it beautiful and bountiful. Unlike most gardens—as it is a photo studio and trial plot—it must look glorious, be healthy, and produce for the kitchen all year. To complicate the maintenance, all the beds are changed at least twice a year. Needless to say, it is a large undertaking. For two decades a quartet of talented organic gardener/cooks have not only given it hundreds of hours of loving attention, but they have also been generous with their vast knowledge of plants. Together we have forged our concept of gardening and cooking, much of which I share with you in this series of garden cookbooks.

I wish to thank Wendy Krupnick for giving the garden such a strong foundation and Joe Queirolo for maintaining it for many years and sharing his view of Italian cooking with me. For decades Jody Main and Duncan Minalga have helped me expand my garden horizons. No matter how complex the project, they enthusiastically rise to the occasion. In the kitchen, I am most fortunate to have Gudi Riter, a very talented cook who developed many of her skills in Germany and France. I thank her for the help she provides as we create recipes and present them in all their glory.

I thank Dayna Lane for her steady hand and editorial assistance. In addition to day-to-day compilations, she joins me on our constant search for the most effective organic pest controls, superior herb varieties, and the best sources for plants.

Gardeners are by nature most generous. I want to thank Carole Saville, who keeps me up to date, and helped with the more esoteric Italian plants and recipes; and Renee Shepherd of Renee's Garden Seeds and Shep Ogden, who are always available to provide vegetable variety information and allow me to prowl their gardens.

I would also like to thank a large supporting cast: my husband, Robert, who gives such quality technical advice and loving support; Nancy Favier for her occasional help in the garden and office; and Susan Freeman for sharing her library of Italian cookbooks, Rayne McGeorge and Deborah Stern for their loving care of my garden.

Many people were instrumental in bringing this book project to fruition. They include Jane Whitfield, Linda Gunnarson, and David Humphrey, who were integral to the initial vision of this book; Marcie Hawthorne for the lovely drawings and Kathryn Sky-Peck. Heartfelt thanks to Eric Oey and to the entire Tuttle staff, especially Deane Norton, Jan Johnson, and Sonia MacNeil, for their help, and to Terri Jadick, June Chong and Irene Ho for bringing this edition to life.

Published by Tuttle Publishing, an imprint of
Periplus Editions (HK) Ltd

www.tuttlepublishing.com

Photographs and Text © 2019 Rosalind Creasy
Illustrations and watercolors by Marcie Hawthorne
Backcover illustration: © ilbusca/istockphoto.com

ISBN 978-0-8048-5201-2
(previously published under ISBN 978-962-593-295-8)

Library of Congress Cataloging-in-Publication Data
in Progess

Revised Edition
23 22 21 20 19
10 9 8 7 6 5 4 3 2 1

Printed in Hong Kong   1903EP

TUTTLE PUBLISHING® is a registered trademark of
Tuttle Publishing, a division of Periplus Editions (HK) Ltd.

Distributed by
North America, Latin America & Europe
Tuttle Publishing
364 Innovation Drive
North Clarendon, VT 05759-9436 U.S.A.
Tel: 1 (802) 773-8930
Fax: 1 (802) 773-6993
info@tuttlepublishing.com
www.tuttlepublishing.com

Japan
Tuttle Publishing
Yaekari Building 3rd Floor
5-4-12 Osaki
Shinagawa-ku
Tokyo 141-0032
Tel: (81) 3 5437-0171
Fax: (81) 3 5437-0755
sales@tuttle.co.jp
www.tuttle.co.jp

Asia Pacific
Berkeley Books Pte. Ltd.
3 Kallang Sector #04-01,
Singapore 349278
Tel: (65) 6741 2178
Fax: (65) 6741 2179
inquiries@periplus.com.sg
www.tuttlepublishing.com

ABOUT TUTTLE:
"Books to Span the East and West"

Our core mission at Tuttle Publishing is to create books which bring people together one page at
a time. Tuttle was founded in 1832 in the small New England town of Rutland, Vermont (USA).
Our fundamental values remain as strong today as they were then—to publish best-in-class books
informing the English-speaking world about the countries and peoples of Asia. The world has
become a smaller place today and Asia's economic, cultural and political influence has expanded,
yet the need for meaningful dialogue and information about this diverse region has never been great-
er. Since 1948, Tuttle has been a leader in publishing books on the cultures, arts, cuisines, languages
and literatures of Asia. Our authors and photographers have won numerous awards and Tuttle has
published thousands of books on subjects ranging from martial arts to paper crafts. We welcome you
to explore the wealth of information available on Asia at **www.tuttlepublishing.com**.